reading the
good book well

reading the good book well

a guide to biblical interpretation

jerry camery-hoggatt

Abingdon Press
Nashville

READING THE GOOD BOOK WELL
A GUIDE TO BIBLICAL INTERPRETATION

This book is printed on acid-free paper.

Library of Congress Cataloging-in-Publication Data

Camery-Hoggatt, Jerry.
 Reading the ood Book well : a guide to biblical interpretation / Jerry Camery-Hoggatt.
   p. cm.
 Includes bibliographical references and index.
 ISBN 978-0687-64275-5 (binding: pbk., lay flat : alk. paper)
1. Bible. N.T.—Hermeneutics.   I. Title.

 BS2331.C36 2007
 220.601—dc22

2007004703

07 08 09 10 11 12 13 14 15 16—10 9 8 7 6 5 4 3 2 1

MANUFACTURED IN THE UNITED STATES OF AMERICA

*For the students, faculty and staff
of Vanguard University,
whom I have dearly loved*

CONTENTS

Contents

Preface

It makes no sense to talk about "reading between the lines" unless first we read the lines themselves.

—C. S. Lewis

I begin this book with a reference to my poor skills as a juggler—three balls is a good show, four is no show at all. Sooner or later someone hands me the one additional ball that brings down the whole act. Yet jugglers sometimes work in troupes, trading off the balls as naturally as if they were extensions of one another. When that happens, though there may be many performers on the stage, still there is only one performance.

So it is with the study of Scripture. If this book shows anything by accident, it is this: The study of the Bible is ultimately a troupe affair. There are simply too many specialties, too many skills, for one person to work the stage alone. We really do need each other.

When I was in seminary, several of my good friends were Anglicans. One or two were even "high church" Anglicans, complete with smells and bells. I was reared in the Pentecostal tradition, a tradition in which worship is nothing if not spontaneous. The contrast between the two forms of worship could not have been more striking, and for this reason I developed a kind of approach-avoidance fascination with the fact that the Anglican liturgy seemed to be so thoroughly prescribed. I wanted to know how that could be an act of worship since it seemed to lack anything at all of individual and spontaneous response to God. I had been tossed a ball I didn't know how to juggle. Eventually, I was relieved of that difficulty by the rector at the church, who deftly stepped in front of me, catching the troubling ball in midair. As we juggled face-to-face, he explained to me that he valued the liturgy because it reminded him that the worship of God was not somehow his own private invention. It was larger than he was, larger than his congregation even; and that it connected us to other worshipers in other times and different places. He was willing to submit himself to the discipline of the liturgy because in doing so he humbled himself before God. That finished, he quietly tossed it back; and, like magic, I was suddenly able to keep this ball going too, along with all the others I was trying to keep in the air. It was a grace-ful trick, a high art.

This is the lesson I have learned about the study of the Bible. It's not our own private business. The very act of studying the Bible connects us with other believers, in other times and different places. We submit ourselves to its disciplines as a way of humbling ourselves before the God who gave us the scriptures in the first place, who summons us to read them, and who meets us there on its pages. Studying the Bible is a troupe affair.

So is writing a book about studying the Bible. The very project connects us to other minds. Several names deserve my thanks. My ever faithful secretary, Christine Williams, assisted with the preparation of the manuscript. Meg Alton made helpful suggestions.

I want to thank especially my daughter, Michal Beth Dinkler, for her careful attention to the details of this manuscript and for her consistently sensible advice. What you find here is much clearer because she read it first.

I am grateful also to my students and to the faculty and staff of Vanguard University. This book is dedicated to them.

PART I

THE WHY OF EXEGESIS

AKA *Prolegomena* (AKA Preliminary Stuff)

In this opening section, we raise preliminary questions about why we study the Bible with such seriousness (chapters 1–2). Chapter 3 raises the larger questions of how competent interpreters, working with identical texts, reach radically different conclusions. We then turn to two preliminary concerns—the manuscripts (chapter 4) and the nature of translation (chapter 5). Stuff like this is called *prolegomena,* which means "preliminary comments."

Chapter 1

READING THE BIBLE AND ACHING FOR GOD

You're conservative, aren't you?" The question was about my theology. The questioner was one of my professors at Boston University, where I was studying for a Ph.D. The professor was a world-renowned sociologist with a heavy European accent, and he liked to buttonhole grad students in public as a way of testing what we were made of.

"Yes, I am," I said. No use pretending. This is what I'm made of. "Then answer me this question," the professor said. He took a puff from his cigarette, then flicked the ashes in my direction. He was enjoying my discomfort. "Why is it that the louder you conservatives are about the inspiration and authority of Scripture, the sloppier you are when you read it?"

Let me comment first about the assumptions that lay behind my professor's question: the question assumes that not all readings of the Bible are equally right, that reading sloppily is a bad thing, and that if we take the inspiration and authority of Scripture seriously we would want to be sure we were reading it well.

In these assumptions he was actually voicing a position that the New Testament itself voices. When I was a boy, a lot of my friends selected "life-verses." A life-verse is a passage of Scripture that serves as a kind spiritual anchor when life gets stormy. Mine was 2 Peter 3:15-16. The subject of the passage is the letters of Paul:

So also our beloved brother Paul wrote to you according to the wisdom given him, speaking of this as he does in all his letters. There are some things in them hard to understand, which the ignorant and unstable twist to their own destruction, as they do the other scriptures.

I chose this verse because I resonated with the statement that there were some things in the letters of Paul that are hard to understand. I've included it here because of the way v. 16 ends. The writer seems to say that it's not enough to study the Bible. It's possible to study it badly, and when we do that, we "twist the Scriptures to our own destruction." At the very least, it means that not all interpretations of the Bible are equally valid. That in turn suggests that we ought to have some way of measuring validity. But of course, this raises the question to which this book is addressed: what does it mean to read the Scriptures properly?

Moving from What the Scriptures *Say* to What They *Mean*

When I was a boy of maybe seven, my family was asked to dinner at the home of a woman in our church who frankly scared me spitless. She was the most refined and elegant woman I knew. She wore Emeraude perfume; she had those high, high shoes with the pointy heels and toes that only refined feet could fit; and she had little diamonds set into the frames of her glasses. I never knew what to say when I was around her, but this time it was worse because we were guests in her home, and it was my very first outing, and my father had warned me to be on my best behavior.

Everything went swimmingly until she served brussels sprouts. I hate brussels sprouts. (No, I *loathe* brussels sprouts.) I didn't eat the ones my hostess served me.

She noticed. She was sitting right next to me, so how could she miss? "Don't you like brussels sprouts?" she asked.

I glanced at my father. He had that look of *fathers-don't-really-care-because-they-know-their-children-will-do-the-right-thing* nonchalance, but he and I both knew it was a mask. He was on his best behavior too.

"Yes, ma'am," I said. "I like 'em fine."

"The boy *loves* brussels sprouts," said my father. He added more to my plate.

I looked hard at my father, hoping he *didn't-really-care-after-all*. He added more to my plate. I looked for the door. My father gave me his clearest *young-man-you-will-sit-there-until-your-plate-is-clean* look. I gulped, I swallowed hard, I stared at the plate, I toyed with the brussels sprouts, I stopped eating the food I liked because it had brussels sprout juice on it, I moved the food around on my plate, but as hard as I might have tried, I couldn't bring myself to put fork to plate to mouth. I didn't eat anything after that. The table conversation moved on to other things. I was home free.

At the end of the evening, the hostess began to clear the table to prepare for dessert. She stopped at my plate.

"I thought you said you liked brussels sprouts," she said.

"I lost my appetite," I said, as quietly as I could, hoping my father wouldn't hear.

"A growing boy like you? No appetite? Not even for brussels sprouts?"

What I said next, I intended as a compliment: "*Sitting next to a woman like you . . .*" I said. Then I foundered. How to compliment my hostess? I really said this: "*Sitting next to a woman like you would make any man lose his appetite.*"

I've told this story here because it illustrates a distinction that stands at the center of what we mean when we talk about interpreting the Bible properly. I didn't mean what my father thought I meant. It isn't enough to ask what the Bible *says*. We also have to ask what it *means*.

Consider for a moment the kinds of things I had to say to him to back out of the trouble I had gotten myself into. I didn't know the sentence had a double meaning. I had read it somewhere and thought it was nice. I wouldn't intentionally insult our hostess.

But these are the sorts of things we take into consideration all the time, whenever we read or listen to people talk. We ask questions like, "Where did this happen? Who said it, and was he smirking at the time? Does this boy usually insult hostesses? Why did he say it that way, and not some other way?" These are the kinds of questions that ordinarily guide our journey from what is *said* to what is *meant*, and they're the same kinds of questions we ought to ask when we read the Bible.

So what my professor was really asking me was, "If you people really think that Scripture is inspired and authoritative, why don't you give it the same kind of attention that you give even the most common language you use every day?"

Surface and Deep Structures

Linguists have their own terms for the distinction between what is said and what is meant. They refer to what is said as the *surface structure* of the language, and what is meant as the *deep structure* of the language. Sometimes a single sentence can puzzle us because it can have two deep structures. Here's an example:

- The chickens are ready to eat.

Depending on context, this may mean that the chickens are in the yard, waiting to be fed, or it may mean that they're in the kitchen, fresh from the oven.

Lots of the joy of language comes from recognizing the subtle interplays that can happen when sentences are ambiguous in this way:

- Librarians are novel lovers.
- I want to die in my sleep like my grandfather. Not screaming and yelling like the passengers in his car.
- "Know what happens when you don't pay your exorcist?"
  "No, what?"
  "You get repossessed."

We can learn something from examples like this: when we encounter ambiguous sentences, we sort through a series of questions, trying to figure out which meaning the speaker intended, or maybe if the speaker intended both. Most Bible scholars think we have to ask the same kinds of questions if we hope to come to right ideas about the meaning of the Bible.

But scholars point out another problem that's logically prior to the question of what the Bible means: before we can come to right ideas about what the Bible *means today*, we first have to understand what it *meant when it was first written*. This is a crucial step that a lot of people skip. In a striking commentary, Harvard chaplain Peter Gomes reflects on the way most of us read the Bible:

> For many the Bible served as some sort of spiritual or textual trampoline: You go onto it in order to bounce off of it as far as possible, and your only purpose in returning to it was to get away from it again.
>
> Bible studies tend to follow this route.... A verse or passage is given out, and the group or class is asked, "What does this mean to

you?" The answers come thick and fast, and we are off into the life stories or personal situations of the group, and the session very quickly takes the form of Alcoholics Anonymous, Twelve-Step meetings, or other exercises in healing and therapy. I do not wish to disparage the very good and necessary work that these groups perform, for I have seen too many good effects and have known too many beneficiaries of such encounter and support groups to diminish by one iota their benefit both to individuals and to the community. I simply wish to say that this is not Bible study, and to call it such is to perpetuate a fiction.[1]

Don't get me wrong here. The scholars aren't saying that the *what-does-this-mean-to-me?* approach is all that wrong. We simply think it's asked too quickly, and that we shouldn't short-circuit important questions about what it meant to its original author and readers.

Different Uses of Scripture

One consideration that can help us be clear about what we're assuming is the distinction between surface structures and deep structures that we looked at earlier in this chapter. We can look at the contexts in which people read the Bible, and then also at the kinds of questions they ask, and then ask what they have in common, in their deep structures.

Homiletics

By *homiletics*, we are referring to the use of Scripture for preaching.

Pastoral Care

Sometimes people come to pastors and theologians hoping for guidance in dealing with some spiritual problem such as an habituated sinful behavior or attitude, or the inability to get past some trauma that has happened to them. Sometimes they're dealing with loss, like the death of a dream or the death of a marriage. Such moments are called *pastoral care*.

Spiritual Direction

Sometimes we ponder Scripture as a way of asking ever deeper and more probing questions about life, and about what God is calling forth in us. If we do this tenaciously, we may find ourselves following a trail of clues to spiritual depth. If we do this in conversation with a guide, we are engaged in *spiritual direction*.

Polity

By *polity* we mean the resolution of questions about the church's legal and organizational life. Questions of polity include such things as membership, voting rights, ordination, ministerial ethics, and so forth. The question of the ordination of women is a matter of polity.

Mission

By *mission* we mean the use of Scripture to define what it is the church is called to be in the world. Is it the mission of the church to make disciples? To lead people to spiritual wholeness? To guarantee the moral core of society? To worship? Is it all of these? None? Some combination of these, or perhaps others?

Ethics

By *ethics* we mean the use of Scripture to provide directives, principles, and examples that can guide our moral decision making. The issues surrounding abortion are issues of ethics.

Apologetics

By *apologetics* we mean the reasoned defense of the faith. Apologetics includes such things as the proof of the reliability of Scripture, defense of the logic of revelation, or the proofs of the existence of God. Issues relating science and the biblical worldview are often addressed apologetically.

Public Theology

By *public theology* we mean the way in which Christians draw upon Scripture in our attempts to affect public attitudes, laws, and policies. This is related to apologetics, but with a different slant: its intention is to evaluate public policies from the standpoint of faith, and to represent the faith in the Great Conversation that takes place in what has been called the Public Square. Advocating for a pro-life political stance is public theology. So is working toward economic justice for the poor.

What Do *These* Have in Common?

Now, the question to ask is, What assumptions do these approaches have in common? What do they share in their deep structures? I will suggest three.

Scripture Is Authoritative

The first commonality here is a deep sense that the Scripture is *authoritative*. By authoritative, we mean that we find it binding in some way. In general conversation, authority has four uses. Sometimes we talk about authority *by virtue of office*. When a police cruiser turns on its flashers behind my car, I pull over because the officer has authority by virtue of office.

A second kind of authority is authority *by virtue of competence*. When I go to my dermatologist to ask about a lesion on my shoulder, I plunk down good money because she is an authority in her field. She has authority by virtue of competence.

A third kind of authority is *moral authority*. If I see a man beating a child, I have a moral obligation to stop him, even though I'm not a policeman, and even though I'm not very good with my fists. (If you look closely at my nose, you will see the marks of one such encounter. I stopped the man as an exercise of moral authority.)

A fourth kind of authority is especially difficult for Americans to grasp: the *authority of a monarch* over his or her people. Recently we had a British guest in our pulpit. He made an interesting distinction between the legal status of Americans and that of the British: "You are *citizens*," he said, "but we are *subjects*." (This is the kind of authority I tried to get my kids to see when I sent them off to bed when they were little. "Why?" they wanted to know. "Because I'm the father, that's why.")

When we make the claim that Scripture is authoritative, we mean all four of these kinds of authority wrapped up together in one. We read the Bible in certain ways because we believe that it makes some kind of claim on us, that it demands we live our lives in a certain way, and that we neglect that demand at our peril.

Scripture Is Inspired

The second thing these uses of Scripture have in common is the notion that Scripture is *inspired*. We sometimes use the word *inspired* in the quite ordinary sense of artful or pleasing or the work of genius. We might say that the music of Mozart or Andrew Lloyd Webber or Sting is inspired in this sense, meaning that it's brilliantly written or performed, pleasing to the ears, beyond the reach of ordinary writers or performers. Much of Scripture is artful in this sense, but that's not what we mean when we say that the Scripture is inspired. Christians have traditionally based our understanding of inspiration on a famous passage in 2 Timothy: "All scripture is *inspired* by God and profitable for teaching, for reproof, for correction, and for training in righteousness, that the man of God may be complete, equipped for every good work" (3:16-17).

In this passage, the word *inspired* is a translation of the Greek word *theopneustos*, which means "God-breathed." When we speak of the inspiration of Scripture, we mean that it possesses revelatory significance, that it provides access to a kind of Truth that cannot be worked out by logic alone or by observation alone or by logic and observation working together.

Scripture Is Sacred

A third commonality of these uses of Scripture is a deep sense that the story told in the Bible is *sacred*. What does it mean to say that something is sacred? This is actually quite difficult to define, so I'd like to try by thinking about the sacred in its smaller, more ordinary sense. What does it mean for *anything* to be sacred to us?

In the book *To a Dancing God*, Sam Keen tells a story about an object that had become sacred to him. The story has three episodes, the first of which was an experience he had when he was a very young boy. One day he and his father were out fishing. To pass the time, his father picked up a peach seed that was lying on the ground, took out his penknife, and carved a tiny monkey. The boy immediately fixated on the monkey—he wanted it more than anything—but his father refused, saying, "This one is for your mother, but I will carve you one someday."[2]

Time went by, and his father forgot and never did carve for him a peach-seed monkey. Eventually the matter was forgotten completely.

The second episode takes place much later in Keen's life. He went to visit his father, who was ill and not expected to live long. They sat on the edge of the desert, under a juniper tree. His father voiced his hesitations about facing the end of his life. Keen recalls, "I heard the right words coming from myself to fill the silence: 'In all that is important you have never failed me. With one exception, you kept the promises you made to me—you never carved me that peach-seed monkey.'"[3]

Episode three: Not long after this conversation, Keen received in the mail a box that contained a peach-seed monkey his father had carved for him. One leg was broken, and there was a note that said, "I'm sorry I didn't have time to carve a perfect one."[4]

Two weeks after he received this package, Keen received word that his father had passed away. The peach-seed monkey instantly became a sacred object to him.

The Sacred stands alongside ordinary reality.

Sometimes when I tell this story to my students at the university where I teach theology, I ask them this question: "If you found a peach-seed monkey at a garage sale or flea market, how much would you be willing to pay for it?" Their answers vary—a nickel, a dime, a penny—but never more than a quarter.

Then I ask, "How much money do you think it would take to get Sam Keen to part with the monkey his father made for him?" Their answers are always something like, "For him, it's priceless, beyond buying and selling." This tells us something important about the sacred: *There is no objective measurement for the worth of the sacred or its role in human life. It stands alongside ordinary reality and provides clues to its deeper meanings; it may be ordinary, but it's also somehow not ordinary.*

This is true of Scripture.

The Sacred connects us to one another.

The peach-seed monkey touched something deep within Keen because it represented an important touchstone with his father.

> For me, a peach-seed monkey has become a symbol of all the promises which were made to me and the energy and care which nourished and created me as a human being. And, even more fundamentally, it is a symbol of that which is the foundation of all human personality and dignity. Each of us is redeemed from shallow and hostile life only by the sacrificial love and civility which we have gratuitously received.[5]

This is also true of Scripture.

The Sacred guides our decision making.

When I was a struggling young professor, trying to repay my academic loans and scrape together enough money to make a down payment on a house, I sometimes reached moments of deep despair. One night my wife and I put the children to bed and then sat in our living room, talking quietly about bankruptcy. We did not know that our six-year-old daughter, Michal Beth, was listening in the hall. When we went to bed that evening, I found a small plastic bag on my pillow with 56 cents in it and a note: "Here, Daddy. It's all I have. Please take it."

Michal Beth is grown and married now, and I still have the bag of coins. I keep it in a drawer in the nightstand beside my bed; and sometimes when I miss her, I take them out and hold them in my hand. The note is barely legible now, but I treasure it in the same way that Sam Keen treasures his peach-seed monkey. It's a holy object to me.

Years later, when Michal Beth told us she wanted to apply to Stanford University, her mother and I sat and considered the consequences of that choice for our future. I got up, went into our bedroom, and from my nightstand I drew out that little bag of coins, held it in my hand, and knew clearly and forcefully what choice I would make. (As they say, "My kid and my money went to Stanford.") Our decision to support Michal Beth's dream wasn't made out of the blue. We still had to consider all sorts of other factors, like where and how we would sustain the family while our finances were tied up in tuition and other costs. We still had to conserve enough resources so we could also provide for her sister and brother. But in the mix, the bag of coins played a huge and probably disproportionate role, not because it obligated us to repay her in kind, but because it is a holy touchstone for something more profound, something I can hardly talk about except by telling the story.

This too is true of Scripture. It's sacred, and for that reason it stands alongside ordinary reality and provides clues to its meaning, it connects us to one another in deep and meaningful ways, and it guides us into truer and more faithful decision making.

Aching for the Sacred

The ache for the sacred lies deep within our core, not as *Christians*, but as *people*. We puzzle over the meaning of our work. Is there a meaning in life beyond simply eating and sleeping and playing video games (or better grades, or faster cars, or newer fashions)? We hope that we can leave the world a better place than it was when we came. The ache for the sacred is somehow central to our humanity itself. This is indeed one of the most important questions, not of our age, but of all ages. Consider the following quote from the novelist, James Michener:

> For this is the journey that men make: to find themselves.... If they fail in this, it doesn't matter much what else they find—money, position, fame, revenge, many loves, are all of little consequence, and when the tickets are collected at the end of the ride, they are tossed into a bin marked "failure." But if a man happens to find himself, if he knows what he can be depended upon to do, the limits of his courage, the positions from which he will no longer retreat ... the extent of his dedication, the secret reservoirs of his determination, the depth of his feelings for beauty, his honest and un-postured goals, then he has found a mansion which he can inhabit all the days of his life.[6]

One of my professors in graduate school once wrote that "the most obvious fact about the contemporary world is not so much its secularity, but rather its great hunger for redemption and for transcendence."[7]

Professor Berger's observation is borne out by my experience at the university. I open one of my classes by asking my students to answer one of the "Quaker Questions": "When did God become more than a word to you?" What is striking to me is that invariably their responses involve some encounter with the sacred. My students have come to be people of faith, not because they were convinced by a watertight refutation of the materialist worldview, but because someone met them and cared for them on a deep level—the level of the sacred and the holy. What they're telling me is their sacred stories.

Christian Faith and the Hunger for the Sacred

Christian faith is just this: it's the proclamation that the whole world has just such a sacred story. This is the real reason we study the Bible. If we do not discover this truth, it little matters what else we find. Christian faith is not a set of moral principles to live by nor a strategy for successful living nor a system of theological abstractions that can be worked out by careful observation and rigid logic. It's not even about getting into heaven. Christian faith is about the discovery that all of us—saint and sinner alike—live in a different reality because of what happened with

Jesus. The incarnation, the birth, the ministry, the death, the crucifixion, the living Christ—all are episodes in a sacred, redemptive story that somehow makes the human experience what it was intended to be. Like the peach-seed monkey, its worth cannot be calculated in dollars and cents, and it points beyond itself to the deeper and more enduring reality that God is at work redemptively in our fallen world. Like Michal Beth's tiny bag of money, it somehow lays its claim upon us and guides us into better and more deeply human decision making.

Theologian Stanley Hauerwas summarizes this reality in the preface of his book *A Community of Character*: "My wish is that this book might help Christians rediscover that their most important social task is nothing less than to be a community capable of hearing the story of God we find in Scripture and living in a manner that is faithful to that story."[8]

Postscript

My professor's question about reading the Bible well did not catch me entirely by surprise. He had asked me this: "Why is it that the louder you conservatives are about the inspiration and authority of Scripture, the sloppier you are when you read it?" He flicked his cigarette and smiled, waiting for my answer. I cleared my throat. "My only answer to you, sir, is that I Am Here."

Chapter 2

IT ISN'T JUST ABOUT GOD; IT'S ALSO ABOUT GARRY

The Problem of Hermeneutics

The student sat pensively across from me, hardly able to look me in the eye. I'll call him Garry. (I've changed his name, as I have the other examples in this book.) He had asked for our meeting, then had spent the better part of the hour talking trivia. How was my work coming? Did I like my new office? His studies were going well. Then—as often happens—when we had stood up to move toward the door, he cleared his throat, averted his eyes, and mumbled something difficult: his wife needed to have an abortion.

I sat back down. "Tell me about that," I said.

Garry reminded me that he had four children, and added something I didn't already know: his wife had twice been hospitalized with severe depression that bordered on suicidal tendencies. Now she was pregnant with their fifth child. The amniocentesis had revealed that the fetus was developing without a brain stem. The doctor had suggested that the most compassionate option was to "return the baby to its maker."

But Garry and his wife were Christians and had strong convictions about abortion. "Returning the baby to its maker" presented them with anguish of a different sort. Would I help him sort through the personal and ethical issues involved?

We talked about consequences of such a decision for his wife, for himself, and for his other children. How would it be if the pregnancy were allowed to come to full term, and then the baby died? Would the trauma of such a loss push his wife beyond her emotional limits? How would an abortion affect her? What if the baby survived? The other children did not know their mother was pregnant. Should he spare them that part of their parents' struggle? If they decided to take the doctor's advice, how would they live with themselves? What good are ethics if we change them to fit the circumstances? What did the Bible say?

Christian Faith Is about Real Life

I have included this story here because it illustrates an important point that is easy to overlook when we talk about interpreting the Bible: *The bottom line is real life.* Chapter 1 surveyed some of the contexts in which Scripture plays a vital role in the lives of individual Christians, congregations, and church bodies—polity, preaching, spiritual direction, Bible study, daily devotions, establishing church mission, defending the faith, pastoral care. In the end, I said that we read the Scriptures in these contexts because we have a sense that it is revealed, that it is authoritative, and ultimately that it tells us the sacred story of redemption. The yearning for the sacred, I said, was the deepest ache of the human heart.

So theology isn't simply about God. It's also about God's dealings with all the Garrys out there who ache for God in the middle of complicated and gut-wrenching circumstances. Let's turn for a moment and examine more closely the contexts in which we use the Bible that were listed in chapter 1.

Homiletics

Homiletics is the *art and science of preaching.* That's the abstraction. The real-life question is, *What should I say as I stand before the congregation to preach the funeral sermon of Elizabeth Marshall? How can I help her family remember her as the gracious and thoughtful woman she was, before the slow anguish of Alzheimer's took her from them?*

Pastoral Care

I defined pastoral care as *counseling and advising, which includes helping people during times of loss or major transition, or in coming to terms with unre-*

solved issues in their spiritual life. That's the abstraction. Sometimes the concrete reality is harder. George came to me after his wife committed suicide following a fight one night. He found her body on the floor in the morning—she had overdosed on sleeping pills. She left him with a two-year-old son. He decided that his life had gone terribly awry and that he should ask again the question of God, so he returned to church. His first Sunday back, the pastor stood in the pulpit and publicly asked for prayer for George: "We all need to pray for George because last week he drove his wife to commit suicide."

George got up, retrieved his son from the nursery, and has never set foot in a church since. How do I now speak to him of grace?

Polity

I defined polity as *the resolution of questions about the church's legal and organizational life.* Do we ordain women? That's the abstraction. In real life, the question is whether we should ordain Carol Simpson, who has long felt the call to ordained ministry, who is a gifted speaker and a thoughtful pastoral caregiver. How will Carol be able to discern that call, and how are we to assist her as she seeks to respond faithfully to the enormous challenges women face in ministry? Does the fact that she is a woman make the discernment process different for her than it is for, say, Patrick Thompson? If we do not ordain women, how will Carol come to terms with her deep sense that she has been summoned by God to a place of ministry?

The point of this illustration is not to argue for or against the ordination of women, but to point out that the way we decide this question will have a direct effect on a real, breathing human being named Carol Simpson.

Ethics, Public Theology, and So Forth

This same comment could be made about the other uses of Scripture—ethics, mission, apologetics, public theology. We could illustrate each one with a hundred stories. What those stories would teach us is that Christians have to live out their faith in very real and sometimes very messy circumstances. As we engage in theological reflection, the messiness is automatically part of the mix. But it's not only that the messiness is there, muddying up our theological thinking, but that the very purpose of our theological thinking involves coming to terms with the messiness, or rather, coming to God in the middle of the messiness. People make life-changing decisions based on what we say—or do not say—in the name of the Bible. The bottom line is about real people, often trying to do what's right—what's *Christian*—in difficult and confusing circumstances.

The Bible Is also about Real Life

But on the other end of the historical continuum, the writers of Scripture were also addressing issues of real life. When Paul writes to Corinth, "Is Christ divided?" (1 Cor 1:13), he's writing to a real congregation that's on the verge of splitting in two. Later in the letter, Paul addresses a moral problem within the Corinthian congregation: A man was sexually involved with his father's wife (5:1-13). Then he turns to another real-life dilemma: Christians were visiting prostitutes and defending that action in the name of grace (6:12-20).

It's fairly easy to see the real-life connections in the Pauline epistles. (After all, epistles tend to be practical documents. We write them to get things done.) What we sometimes overlook is that the other documents of the Bible were also written to real people in real-life situations. Mark and Hebrews were written to congregations that were under persecution. Luke wrote to a congregation that was divided over ethnic relations. Matthew appears to have been written to a congregation in which Jewish Christians were abandoning their new faith and returning to the older, non-Christian Judaism of their parents and grandparents.

The Problem of Particularity

In this way we're introduced to something theologians sometimes call *the problem of particularity*. Whenever we read Scripture we are builders of bridges between there and then, and here and now. If this is so, the bridges we build are almost always buttressed on both ends by real-life situations and not by general principles. The particular on this end has to be correlated in some way with the particular on that end.

Historical-Cultural Distance

When we compare the real-life questions of people today with the real-life questions asked by the people in the Bible, we encounter another problem: *Real life is slippery.* It's constantly changing out from under us. Not only do we seek guidance from the Scriptures for situations that the writers of Scripture did not intend, we seek that guidance in a world the writers of Scripture could never have imagined.

How would it be if we could go back in time and discuss our problems with one of the great saints of the church? For a moment, imagine explaining Garry's dilemma about abortion to doctor Luke. What would Luke make of amniocentesis? How would he understand the issues surrounding heart-lung transplants? brain-wave activity? stem-cell research? Is there a religious and spiritual dimension to heart transplants, and how is the Bible to be a helpful guide in deciding the morality of that? Recently I read of a woman who served as surrogate mother to her own grandchild. How would Luke understand that, and would he consider it moral?[1] How would we explain to Paul the whole problem of dirty bombs or weapons of mass destruction? What would Matthew make of computer identity theft? global warming? the ozone layer? Internet pornography? crack cocaine?

The problem of historical-cultural distance cuts both ways. Christians in the first century were wrestling with real-life issues that most of us never think about. What to do about meat offered to idols or competing explanations of the incarnation, such as that which emerged in Gnosticism? What about the syncretistic claim that Jesus is divine; sure, but just another god among others in a whole pantheon of gods?

Theologians call this slipperiness *historical-cultural distance*. We are apt to think of historical-cultural distance as a problem to be overcome, and in a sense it is. But it's also a resource. If we listen well, we may discover that we can hear voices that do not share our narrow, mechanistic worldview, or our fragmenting view of individualism at all costs. We may hear prophetic voices that thunder down the centuries, calling us to a more radical commitment to justice. We may hear poetic voices that sing against the gods of the world—their world and, incredibly, our world too—and call us to a purer vision of life.

The Problem of Hermeneutics

When we combine these two problems—particularity and historical-cultural distance—we arrive at what scholars call *the problem of hermeneutics*. (Hermes was the Greek name of Mercury, the Roman god with wings on his shoes who—like the FTD florists who use Mercury as their logo—

19

delivered the messages of the gods.) The Greek word *hermeneuo* means, "I interpret," or "I translate." *Hermeneutics* can therefore be called "the art and science of interpretation." *Hermeneutics* is not particularly a theological word. Philosophers talk a lot about the hermeneutics of all kinds of texts. In the interpretation of the Bible, we need to make a small adjustment: Hermeneutics involves reading the text properly, then applying it in circumstances for which it may not have been intended.

So what we have is a kind of journey, which we could represent with a diagram:

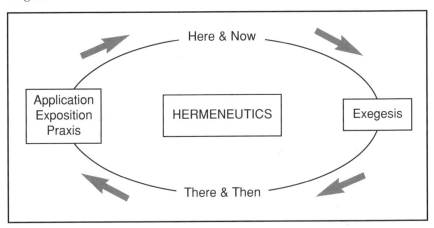

Figure 2.1: The Problem of Hermeneutics

Exegesis

For clarity, we define the problem of hermeneutics as two different movements. In the first, we ask, "What did the text mean *there and then?* What did the author mean, and how would his text have been understood by the readers he had in mind when he wrote?" We call this first step *exegesis*. Someone who does exegesis is called an *exegete*.

Exposition/Application/Praxis

The return journey asks, "What does this text mean *here and now?*" This second step is called by a variety of names—sometimes *exposition*, sometimes *application*, and sometimes *praxis*.

Whatever we call this second movement, it seems clear that it logically follows the first movement. Before we can apply the Bible, first we have to understand it, and while we do not change our exegesis to fit our application, we do change the application to fit the exegesis. (One way to say this is that exegesis is *controlling* for application, but not the other way around.) We have to hold the application part more loosely, at least until we've finished the exegesis part.

An Experiment in Hermeneutics

Suppose we take a concrete example. In 1 Timothy 5:23, Paul tells Timothy to "No longer drink only water, but use a little wine for the sake of your stomach...."

Exegesis asks the question of what the text meant in its original context. First, wine in the first century was usually cut with water in a 1:4 ratio—four parts water to one part wine. In the absence of modern distilling techniques, the uncut wine could achieve about 9 percent alcohol content by volume, so we're not looking at a direct transfer of meaning from the Greek word *oinos* to the English word *wine*. The terms overlap, but not precisely. The Ancients never heard of Smirnoff 100 proof. Second, it appears that Timothy was getting sick from drinking his water uncut. In the first century, no one knew about micro-organisms, but they did know that if you cut your water with a little wine, you were less likely to get sick from it. The alcohol in the wine would purify the water by killing the microbes, like the halizone tablets we used to put in our canteens when we were Scouts. So this passage appears to be about the medicinal use of alcohol, not about drinking generally. Paul is encouraging Timothy to use a little common sense.

Application asks how we should hear this text today, given what it meant there and then. Suppose a youngster in the church youth group discovers this text and assumes that it contains a blanket approval of drinking. (Indeed, a literalist could make the case that all Christians should drink wine.) But would that be a right use of Scripture? A more responsible interpretation would recognize the limits of what the text actually says in its own context, and then would ask how the realities of the modern world may call for a different set of limits. Perhaps the closest parallel should be "if you're getting sick from the tap water, try using a water purifier." Perhaps our appropriation of this text should take into account the fact that we have heavy machinery to operate (including automobiles!). In the first century, if you drank too much at a party, the worse that could happen to you on the way home is that you might fall off your donkey.

To Sum Up

If this chapter has any take-away value for you, I hope it's this: First, we can't just apply the text any way we want. Whatever we say about what the Bible means here and now has to be controlled by what it meant there and then. I hope you can see, second, that the application of the text isn't always direct and automatic, but calls for careful thought, not only about the world in which the text was first *written* but also about the world in which it is being *applied*. I hope you'll see, third, that this isn't about abstractions disconnected from real life. In fact it's about the opposite. What we believe about the Bible and about God can radically change the way we live, who we associate with, how we make decisions, what we hope for, where we look to find answers to the troubles we inevitably face. Finally, when you put all of these observations together, I hope you'll see that it's worth taking time to think carefully about what we're doing when we interpret this ancient and holy book.

It appears that a bare, direct, unilateral application of the text may not be adequate as we shift from one culture to another. So how do we make that journey? Do all Christians agree about how that process works? Is there some way to sort through the wide range of interpretations, looking for a common denominator?

We turn to these questions in chapter 3.

Postscript

Garry and his wife were considering an abortion because the fetus was severely deformed. I told him that whatever choice they made, he and his family would remain in my prayers. Then I suggested that before they took a step as drastic as abortion, they should seek a second opinion, maybe even a third. They did. The second opinion disproved the first. The baby was born later that year, a fine, healthy boy.

Chapter 3

THE BIBLE SAYS IT; I BELIEVE IT; THAT SETTLES IT—OH, REALLY?

Introducing Paradigms

C hapter 2 suggested that the meaning of the text today has to be controlled by the meaning the text held for its original writers and readers. Our *application* has to be controlled by our *exegesis*. What this means is that exegesis is like the foundation, and application is like the house. What happens if we build a house on a faulty foundation? The walls crack, the house crumbles, and we find ourselves ducking falling timber.

That's easy enough to say but harder to do because the claims people make about the meaning of the Bible aren't all equally valid. Consider the way the King James Version translates Jesus' words of institution of the Last Supper in Matthew 26:27:

> And he took the cup, and gave thanks, and gave it to them, saying, *Drink ye all of it.*

When I was a young man, I was confused to hear conflicting sermons based on two very different interpretations of this verse. One preacher interpreted *drink ye all of it* as, "drink everything in the cup," while the other preacher said it meant, "every one of you, drink from it."[1] Were they both right? If one was right and the other wrong, how would I know?

But It Just *Feels* Right . . .

It would be an interesting study to find out, not how people reached incorrect interpretations but how they came to believe that those incorrect interpretations were right. I suspect that a major reason we do this is that when we consider a new interpretation, we stop when we reach one that *feels* right. The problem here is that the feeling of rightness isn't a very reliable criterion of validity.

Sometimes my students ask me this question: What if the *feelings* are really the leading of the Holy Spirit? My answer is threefold. First, what if they're not? How would you know? What do you say to two different interpreters who both *feel* that the Holy Spirit has inspired their interpretation, but their two readings of the Scripture are incompatible? The answer to this question is that we judge our sense of the leading of the Spirit against the witness of Scripture, and not the other way around. That moves the question back to square one: What does the Scripture say? Indeed, if the Holy Spirit functioned in this particular way, we wouldn't need a Bible. We could all just listen to what the Spirit was saying, and obey the promptings of our inner life.

Second, there is no *inspired* translation of the Bible. We're now able to read the Bible only because somebody took careful pains to do the careful work of exegesis.

Third, sometimes what we find in Scripture reflects our own fears and biases, or our place in the history of culture. This is clear in historical retrospect, but less clear when we're in the middle of some historical moment. In the nineteenth century, Christians in England were forced to come to terms with new and sometimes wonderful inventions: what to make of advances in science and medicine, for example. At that time, patients who had to undergo surgery were subject to excruciating pain. Doctors would strap them to the operating table, and then cut and saw away—a terrifying ordeal. Then a Scottish doctor named Sir James Simpson decided it would be a good and compassionate thing to find some relief for this suffering, and so began a series of experiments, using himself and fellow physicians as guinea pigs. On November 4, 1887, they sniffed from a vial of chloroform crystals—and promptly passed out unconscious. Problem solved.

Or was it? Almost immediately the new anesthetic was condemned by church leaders on the grounds that freedom from pain was only to be found in heaven, and therefore it was both immoral and unchristian to try and escape pain while we're still on earth.[2] Felt right then; feels wrong today.

The history of the church is filled with similar stories. Some nineteenth century theologians argued that Christians should not use subways because to do so would bring us closer to the underworld, and in that way expose us to the workings of the devil. In the same way, some twentieth century church leaders argued that Christians should not preach the gospel over the radio because radio waves were in the air, and who was the devil but the prince of the powers of the air?

What these men were arguing doesn't seem very sensible today; but to them, when they made those arguments, they seemed wonderfully clear and compelling. What this means is that the internal sense of rightness isn't a very good measure of whether or not we've understood the Bible or applied it properly. We have to have a different yardstick for that.

There's a dark side of this discovery that good intentions by themselves don't necessarily make for valid reading. The *right* interpretation just might feel *wrong* for a while, and we can't use those feelings of wrongness as a reason to take a given interpretation off the table. We need a more reliable standard than that. If you eat canned peas long enough, fresh peas taste funny. That's why sometimes the business of learning new things about the Bible requires an act of moral courage as we patiently consider all the options.

So What Happened, Anyway?

If we look carefully at the history of interpretation, we can see several major patterns in what people did and why they did it.

Serving Our Own Predispositions

First, we learn that interpreters don't come to the Bible as blank books. We come with vested interests, commitments, ideas about what can and can't happen, and ideas about what should and shouldn't happen. Sometimes our personal and national histories contribute to the bias. We want the Bible to read a certain way. Before the American Civil War, slave owners in the South emphasized the positive instructions the Bible gives to slaves:

> Slaves, be obedient to those who are your earthly masters, with fear and trembling, in singleness of heart, as to Christ; not in the way of eyeservice, as men-pleasers, but as servants of Christ, doing the will of God from the heart, rendering service with a good will as to the Lord and not to men, knowing that whatever good any one does, he will receive the same again from the Lord, whether he is a slave or free. (Eph 6:5-8)

But they ignored the instructions given to Christian slave owners: "Masters, do the same to them, and forbear threatening, knowing that he who is both their Master and yours is in heaven, and that there is no partiality with him" (v. 9).

If we come wanting the text to mean some particular thing, what we want it to mean can distort our understanding the way iron distorts the readings of a compass.

Starting from the Wrong Presuppositions

Second, we learn that some interpreters begin with the wrong presuppositions. By *presuppositions* we mean the *a priori* assumptions that are required if the interpretation is to be logical. (*A priori* means "in advance.") These concern the limits of what is and isn't possible. (It's a presupposition of logic that "A cannot be non-A.") Because they are *a priori*, such assumptions aren't proved by logic or experiment. They must be in place beforehand if logic is to function as a way of demonstrating some conclusion. A good example of a presupposition is the conviction that miracles do not, did not, cannot happen. A competing presupposition is that if the Bible says there were miracles, then by God there were miracles. The God who made the world out of nothing ought to be pretty good on spare parts.

The point here is that if I change my presuppositions, I change the results of my interpretation.

Supplying the Wrong Background Information

Third, we learn that some interpreters read the text against the wrong background information. By *background information* I mean the cultural information that is necessary if the interpreter is to fill in the gaps in the evidence and organize the parts into a coherent and meaningful whole. All interpretation requires that we bring in outside information, and the manner in which we do that dramatically changes the conclusions we are likely to reach.

Many years ago my wife and I attended a large church that was building a new sanctuary. The pastor, being a thoughtful man, read widely in the literature of church fund-raising, hoping to learn as much as he could about how to address the special needs of a congregation that has undertaken this challenge. One of the books was a fund-raiser's guide, written by a well-known church consultant. At the same time as the pastor read this book, he delivered a series of sermons on the OT book of Nehemiah, who was involved in a building project of his own—restoring the walls of Jerusalem after the return from exile in Babylon. The strange thing was that every major principle the pastor preached from the book of Nehemiah he had first found in the consultant's fund-raising manual.

Following the Wrong Protocols

Finally, history teaches us that some interpreters follow the wrong protocols. By *protocols* I mean the ordered steps—the "interpretive conventions"—of research itself. These include analogies from similar examples, the sequence in which we do our study, our habits of thought. A good example is the ordered sequence of steps you follow when you troubleshoot a problem setting up your Internet account. The steps follow a logical sequence; and if you get the sequence wrong, you may have trouble locating and fixing the problem. The results of each step "indicate" what next steps to follow. Here, as elsewhere, the sequence of steps is an important factor in responsible research.

Consider for a moment what the pastor did in the previous example. If he had done his exegesis of Nehemiah first, and read the church fund-raising literature second, he might have preached a very different series of sermons. By following the sequence he did, he inadvertently blocked out Nehemiah's own distinctive voice. He also elevated the fund-raiser's manual to the level of Scripture, at the same time reducing Nehemiah to the level of illustration. By preaching this way, he gave the manual an authority it did not really possess. What member of his congregation could stand up then and say, "Let's try a different approach"?

Introducing Paradigms

I admit it: I haven't been playing fair with you. There's an assumption built into my discussion. I've been assuming that there's a *right* kind of predisposition, a *right* kind of prior information, *right* protocols, and *right* presuppositions.

These are the four basic parts of any interpretive method. The technical name for a method of study that defines its presuppositions, prior information, predispositions, and protocols is *paradigm*. This is a grand term, kicked about a lot lately. We get this term from the work of an historian of science named Thomas Kuhn.[3] In the rest of this chapter we tap briefly into Kuhn's analysis because it explains how the processes of research influence conclusions.

Kuhn began by observing that science doesn't develop smoothly through the gradual accumulation of data, but rather with fits and starts and through dramatic revolutions of thought. This is very different from the common idea that scientists simply collect more and more information and add it to the store of information that already exists. According to Kuhn, science moves forward by *re*-volution, not *e*-volution. The fact that we no longer believe that the world is flat is the result of a major revolution in scientific thought.

How does this happen? Kuhn's explanation is that scientific revolutions occur because of an aspect of scientific observation itself: The scientific mind is trained to observe in a particular way. The collection of data is guided by the scientist's training, his or her skills of observation, intentions, habits of mind, tools, methods of collecting data and keeping records, and the range of available contextual information. In practice this means two things: This means, first, that the scientist comes to the data with a paradigm already in hand, and second, that the paradigm limits what the scientist is likely to see.

This, then, is what paradigms do: They enable interpretation to take place, but they do so only by imposing structure and pattern on the collection and interpretation of the facts. This can be demonstrated quite graphically. Scientists have long used visual tools to illustrate the role of the mind in discovering patterns in what we see. One such image is the following photograph:

Figure 3.1

The image is a high-contrast photograph of a dalmatian dog. The dog is facing away from the camera, nose to the ground in the dead center of the photograph. Many observers have difficulty seeing the image at first, but once they have seen it, they can recall or dismiss it at will. The eye can bring it in and out of focus. The capacity for bringing the image into focus depends upon the mind's activity of organizing the details on the image in a particular kind of relationship to one another. To do this, the mind must heighten some elements of the image and overlook other elements. But on what basis? The mind can only make those decisions by bringing in outside information—what it knows about dalmatians.

A different image but to similar effect is noted in figure 3.2:

Figure 3.2

This image is a drawing of a woman. Some observers will see a young woman, wearing a choker around her neck. She is facing away from the observer, and the line of her jaw can be easily traced along the center of the picture. Other people will more naturally see an older woman, facing forward and gazing slightly to the left of the picture. The line that was the young woman's jaw here becomes the shadow line of the old woman's nose. The choker becomes her mouth.

Everything depends upon how one organizes the parts. At the very least, this means that what we see depends in part on what we bring to the seeing. Kuhn would say that it depends on the paradigm we use. Once we've seen both women, it's quite easy to toggle back and forth between them. The interpretive possibilities lie not only in the lines on the page but also in the way the mind chooses to organize the lines into meaningful patterns. This is what happens whenever we interpret anything. Paradigms enable interpretation to take place, but they do so by imposing structure and pattern on the observation and collection of data.

For the paradigm to be useful, it must enable the observer to manage the data responsibly and sensibly. This means that in scientific research the value of a paradigm can be judged according to its ability to explain observable evidence and to enable reliable predictions about the results of experimentation. The more adequate the paradigm, the more it is able to account for reality with precision and scope. Where two paradigms can explain the same phenomena with equal precision and equal scope, the simpler of the two is to be preferred.

So science doesn't evolve smoothly; it lurches forward. An excellent illustration is Copernicus's discovery that the world goes around the sun, rather than the other way around. It wasn't simply that there was additional information that had to be accounted for, but that the earlier way of accounting itself turned out to be wrong. Copernicus revisits the old calculations, Galileo looks through his telescope, Sir Francis Bacon makes some adjustments to the model, and together they manage to move the world out of the center of the universe, and hang it in a moving trajectory around a minor star. This is not so much developing the older model as it is turning the older model out to pasture.

We would see the same thing if we were to survey the history of the interpretation of the Bible. Paradigm shifts have called for the radical transformations in a variety of disciplines, including theological study. Sometimes human understanding changes by revolution—even by violent revolution—rather than by gradual adaptation of a working model. So the history of science looks like this:

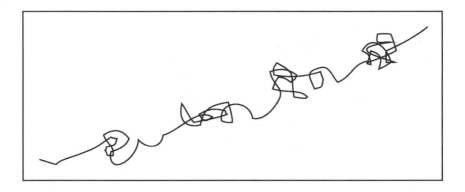

Figure 3.3

Kuhn was interested in the messy moments of the process, when the accepted models of reality are thrown into question, but newer models are not yet fully formed. That's why he called his book, *The Structure of Scientific Revolutions*.

Paradigms Must Be *Critical*

It follows then that the clearer we are about the limitations of our paradigms the less likely we will be to use them badly. A paradigm that has been rigorously examined is called *critical*. By *critical* we don't mean hostile, but something more like "*self*-critical," or more precisely, "aware of its own strengths and limitations." We have a better chance of reaching valid conclusions if we put our working paradigm out on top of the table where we can see its strengths and limitations.

I had a friend in college who discovered that there are a variety of ways in which Christians think through questions of morality. At the same time, he discovered the problem of historical-cultural distance in interpreting the biblical text. As he began working through these issues, he slipped into a terribly destructive pattern of behavior—he began sleeping with his girlfriend.

One day, I confronted him.

"You're a Christian. How can you do that?"

He appealed to the problem of hermeneutics: "The world is different now," he said. "In the Bible, they didn't have the pill, and they didn't have penicillin, so we're in a different cultural context. New rules for a new situation."

I answered that his appeal to historical-cultural distance might make sense if the purpose of marriage was to prevent unwanted pregnancies and venereal disease, but that there was a whole lot more to marriage than that.

"I love her. That's enough." (In this he was appealing to a system of ethics called *situation ethics*, though I do not think he was willing to think this through very carefully.)

"If you love her, why not marry her?"

"Because I'm not sure I'll always love her," he said.

"Then you run a risk of hurting her somewhere down the line. You could do this girl serious damage. How then can you say that you love her?"

"Because if we break up and she's somehow damaged by that, she'll grow through that experience of loss."

This conversation actually took place. I've included it here to point out that my friend was bright enough that he could shift his thinking about ethics around like stepping-stones until he found a path that led to exactly what he would have done if he had had no ethics at all. Ethics, if they are to be true ethics, must be set out in advance; and they must ask more of us than we would ask of ourselves. In the same way, if we set out our interpretive paradigm before we begin our study, we will be more likely to hear the text when it says things we might not have been willing or able to think of on our own.

Paradigms Must Be *Collegial*

My conversation with my friend illustrates another point: We're helped by discussion with people who don't share our points of view. The truth is, none of us is omniscient, and when there's something we don't know, sometimes we don't know that we don't know it. When we study the Bible in a community, we increase the pool of knowledge we can draw upon. The more people in that community, and the better informed those people are, the greater the chance that someone else in the group will be able to supply critical information we may not have known we were missing.

Paradigm Theory and Biblical Studies

Paradigm theory also helps us understand the present situation in biblical studies. If we diagram paradigm change in science, we may get something that looks like figure 3.3. If we diagram paradigm change in the study of the Bible, what we get is much more complicated:

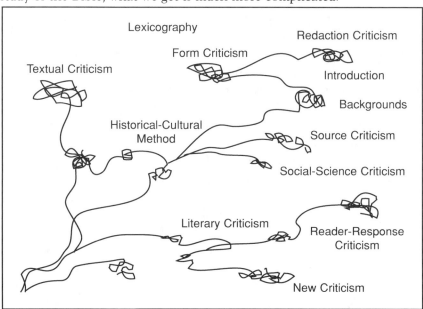

Figure 3.4

How do we explain this complexity? In *science*, we can apply objective, measurable criteria to validate the paradigm we are using. We ask questions like this:

- Does this hypothesis enable us to predict the results of experiment?
- Are the measurements accurate?
- Are the results repeatable?
- Does it explain the observable evidence with precision and scope?
- Is it consistent with what we know from other scientific research?

This means that there are specific, identifiable ways that scientific conclusions can be validated, and specific ways in which it can be refuted.

But in theological studies, criteria such as these are less helpful. We can't really rely on experimentation to check our results. The results are open to challenge from a lot of directions, and people naturally defaulted to interpretations that made sense to them without asking if the interpretations could be validated in some other way.

Within the technical study of the Bible, a number of different paradigms developed, each one intending to examine a different aspect of the Bible. As a result, the technical study of the Bible developed along a variety of different lines.

Look again at figure 3.4. Here's the temptation: Why not pick out the paradigm that feels right and master that, then treat it as though it's the only one? There are two problems with doing that. First, the various paradigms are designed to answer different kinds of questions. If we use only one paradigm, but then claim that the result equals the whole study of the Bible, we commit the logical error of confusing a part with the whole. This is like finding a wheel and calling it a cart. Second, since paradigms focus attention—and therefore suppress attention—if we use only one paradigm, we automatically miss stuff that only the other paradigms tell us. If that other stuff is important, our results are skewed.

So Which Paradigms Are *Safe*?

Sometimes at the university where I teach theology, my students will ask me to direct them to the "safe" theological literature. I think that what they're looking for is literature that will confirm the interpretation of the Bible they already have, rather than challenge them to think through the questions from a fresh perspective or with different information in hand. They're looking for interpretations that *feel* right, given what they already believe.

Sometimes to answer this question, I stand behind my podium and ask my students if they can see my notes, which of course they can't. They see only the front of the podium, while I see the sloping surface that faces me. I see all of their faces, while they mostly see the backs of other students' heads. There is no single vantage point that gives a person a universal perspective. I tell my students that we stand to learn more from people who are different from us than from those who are like us. The recognition that we need each other is a statement of humility, a frank recognition that only God is omniscient.

Is There a Right Paradigm for Exegesis?

I think there's a better way to approach this question: Is it possible to create a paradigm specifically to recover the author's intention?

The answer to that question is that it's not only possible, but relatively straightforward: We would design a paradigm that replicated the activities the authors expected their readers would engage in. More precisely, such a paradigm would replicate the *prior information* the original reader is expected to have in hand; it would read from the standpoint (or *predispositions*) of the original reader; it would respect the *protocols*, or reading conventions for which the text was designed, and it would respect the worldview (or *presuppositions*) the writer expected his reader to share.

We will turn to these questions in chapter 6. First we have to take a detour: Before we can think about what a text *means*, first we have to determine what a text *says*. That means examining the manuscripts very carefully to reconstruct the correct wording. Then we make a preliminary translation, or pick out a translation to use as our base. We turn to these matters in chapters 4 and 5.

So How Do I Find Out More about This Topic?

Lots of work here. I'll just mention four: Thomas Kuhn, *The Structure of Scientific Revolutions* (Chicago: University of Chicago Press, 1970);

Cordell Strug, "Kuhn's Paradigm Thesis: A Two-Edged Sword for the Philosophy of Religion," *Religious Studies* 20 (1984): 269-79; Margaret Masterman, "The Nature of a Paradigm," in *Criticism and the Growth of Knowledge* (ed. Imre Lakatos and Alan Musgrave; Cambridge: Cambridge University Press, 1970), 59-89; Hans Kung and David Tracy, eds., *Paradigm Change and Theology* (New York: Crossroad, 1991).

Chapter 4

Reconstructing the Original Wording

The Discipline of Textual Criticism

A ll right, so we've decided that we want to know what the authors of the Bible meant by what they wrote. Before we can do that, we first have to figure out what words they wrote. This poses a problem because we have thousands of manuscripts in Greek and many more than that in ancient translations. If we compare these with one another, we discover variations in almost every verse, every sentence. It's estimated that there are as many as 300,000 variant readings of NT texts. No two manuscripts agree at every point.

Sometimes the problem of the variations in manuscript evidence comes up quite unexpectedly. A member of the youth group discovers that the last twelve verses of Mark have been set off by brackets, with a notation in the margin that reads something like: *Verses 9-20 are not found in the better manuscripts*. A similar note is found in the well-known story of the woman taken in adultery found (in some manuscripts!) in John 7:53–8:11. Try asking someone in your Bible study group to look up John 5:4.

To solve problems like this, biblical scholars have developed a special-ized paradigm (or "discipline") called *Textual Criticism*. Experts in this field are called *text critics*. (Let me warn you in advance: This is a roll-up-your-sleeves chapter. Be prepared.)

Imagine for a moment that there is no New Testament. No King James Version, no NIV, no RSV. Zip. Nada. One day you're out digging around in some ancient crypt, and you come upon a trove of manuscripts. (Some of them are really old, so your first thought is, "We're rich!") They're written in Greek, but you know Greek so you're OK with that. The manuscripts all seem to be handwritten copies of the same book, or maybe a small library of books. There are over five thousand of them, so you have to do some heavy sorting.

You start by sorting them into categories. Some seem to contain a kind of heading, *kata Matthaion*, so you put these all in the same pile. Some start with *kata Markos*. Another pile. So it goes. Then you start comparing the *kata Matthaion* manuscripts with one another. This is where you get frustrated. They tell the same story, but they differ in the ways they tell it. Sometimes the differences are quite major, and other times they're just differences of spelling. Some manuscripts contain words or phrases that are missing in other manuscripts.

This is precisely where we are with the manuscripts of the NT, except that we didn't find them all in one place, and we've known about them for a long long time. The challenge we face is finding a way to get back to the wording of the original.

Enter Textual Criticism

Text critics work directly from the Greek manuscripts, and because they need to be precise they use very technical vocabulary, so let's begin with some definitions.

Autograph

We use the word *autograph* to mean the very first manuscript, the one that came from the pen of the author. For reasons that will become clear in a moment, we can be certain that the autographs of the New Testament are lost.

Codex, Scroll

We use the word *codex* to describe a manuscript that is set up in page format, and the word *scroll* to mean *scroll*.

Manuscript

We use the word *manuscript* to refer to a handwritten copy. (The root word here is the Latin, *manus*, which means "hand.") The abbreviation for *manuscript* is *ms* (plural: *mss*).

Siglum

Most of the important mss are identified by a name and a *siglum* (or "sign"). The plural of *siglum* is *sigla*. For example, the siglum for Codex Alexandrinus is capital letter A; for Codex Vaticanus, B; for Codex Bezae Cantabrigiensis, D.

Here's an example of an early ms. This one's named Papyrus Bodmer XV, and it carries the siglum P[75]. (The letter P stands for *Papyrus*.) P[75] dates from between AD 175 and 225.

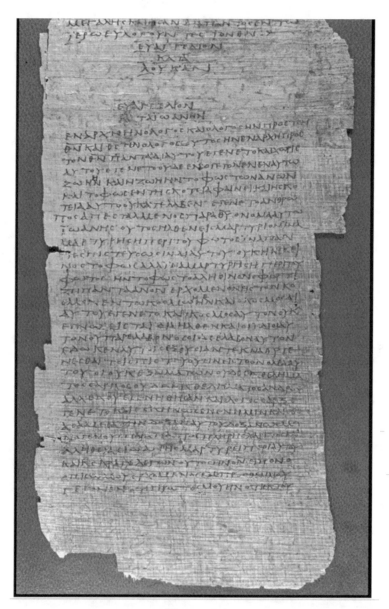

Figure 4.1

Scribe/Copyist

By these two terms we mean the person doing the copying. (I prefer to use the term *copyist* consistently for this because a lot of people get the word *scribe* confused with the Jewish scribes who were opposed to Jesus' ministry. For most of the history of hand-copying of the Bible, the copyists were Christian monks working in monasteries.)

Text

By *text* we mean the wording found on a ms. In this very narrow sense, the text isn't even the ink with which the wording is recorded, but is instead the wording itself. This is a very important distinction. Almost all statements of faith that affirm that the Bible is inspired or authoritative make that statement very carefully: "The Bible is inspired (or inerrant, or infallible) in the *text* of the autographs." The distinction between a text and a manuscript is what makes it possible to say that the *autograph* may be lost, the *text* is not. Almost certainly, the *text* of the autograph can be reconstructed.

Variant

We use the term *variant* to mean one of the options wherever the mss differ from one another.

Textual Criticism/Lower Criticism

Let's refine our definition: *Textual Criticism* is that discipline of study designed to recover the *text* of the *autographs* by careful comparison of the differences in the *manuscripts*. (Sometimes in the older theological literature, this discipline is called *lower criticism*, to distinguish it from *higher criticism*, which is the study of the historical implications of the text.)

To Restate the Problem, Then . . .

Suppose we take a single verse as an example. For this exercise, I've selected Luke 10:37. To make the matter clear, I'll translate three different manuscripts. For clarity, I'll add the siglum for each ms at the beginning of each line

A	But it happened that as
P^{75}	And as
B	And as

A	they journeyed they entered a certain village a woman
P[75]	they journeyed they entered a certain village a woman
B	they journeyed they entered a certain village a woman

A	named Martha invited him into her house
P[75]	named Martha invited him
B	named Martha invited him

A	and her sister Maria was there
P[75]	and her sister Mariam was there
B	and her sister Maria was there

The Claremont Profile Method

But this could be displayed more conveniently. Suppose we put all the places where the mss agree on a single line, then make a bubble for each place where they disagree. This method of displaying variations is called *The Claremont Profile Method* because it was developed at the Institute for Antiquity and Christianity in Claremont, California.

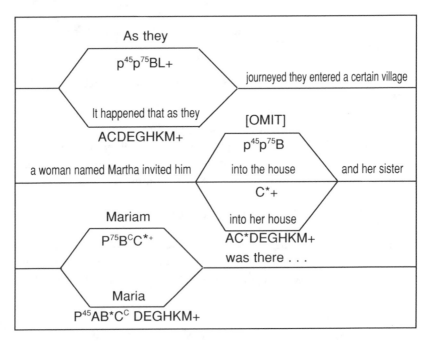

Figure 4.2

In this diagram, each bubble represents a *variation unit*, and each option within a bubble represents a *variant reading*. (The asterisks [*] indicate original readings, and the superscript c [ᶜ] indicates that a correction has been made.)

Types of Copyist Errors

How does this happen? Surprisingly, the huge number of copyist errors turns out to be a happy problem to have because the mistakes fall into patterns. The basic strategy text critics use is to identify these patterns and then reverse engineer them to get to the text of the original. There are three basic types of errors:

- •Errors of Sight
- •Errors of Hearing
- •Errors of Mind

Errors of Sight

The most common mistakes are errors of sight. Look closely at the following ms.

Figure 4.3

43

As you look, notice the following things:

- *The words are all run together.* This is like word wrap carried to the next level.
- *There's very little punctuation.*
- *There are no chapter and verse divisions.*
- *Sometimes the handwriting is sloppy.*

IT'SEASYTOSEEHOWACOPYISTMIGHTMAKEMISTAKESINTHECASEOFTHENTTHE
PROBLEMISCOMPOUNDEDBECAUSESOMEOFTHEMSSAREQUITEOLDANDSOME-
TIMESTHECOPYINGWASNOTNEATORCAREFULORTHEINKHASWORNOFFTHEP-
AGEANDBECAUSESOMEMSSARETORNORDAMAGEDINSOMEWAYBESIDESITSREA
LLYDIFFICULTTOREADSOMETHINGTHATSWRITTENWITHOUTWORDBREAKS-
STANDARDIZEDSPELLINGORVERYMUCHPUNCTUATION.

It's pretty easy to see how copyists might make errors of sight. Add to that the fact that nobody had glasses, lighting was often poor, and print-ing was sometimes sloppy. Here's an example I read once in *Reader's Digest*:

> My roommate at Bethel College ... had received a cake in the mail and didn't have a chance to eat any because he was leav-ing for the weekend. He left me a hastily scrawled note telling me his plans, ending with "take cake."
>
> Happy with his generosity, I enjoyed the treat, finishing most of it by the time he had returned. He seemed very disappointed that there was only one small piece left for him. When I reminded him of his note, he shook his head and said, "It doesn't say 'take cake,' it says, 'take care.'"

Take a clue from this illustration: The wording "take cake" made sense because there was a cake sitting on the counter. If there had been no cake, the reading would have been puzzling, and the reader would have checked. This leads to a small principle: If a copying error makes sense, it goes unnoticed. If the error doesn't make sense, the copyist will have an internal prompt to check to see that he got it right.

There are several common errors of sight:

- Confusing letters that look alike.
- Copying a word or letter twice (*dittography*), or omitting a word or letter (*haplography*).
- Dropping a line because it looks similar to a line already copied (*homoioteleuton*)

Errors of Hearing

Here's a way to speed the way we make copies: Station a reader (called a *lector*) at a podium at the front of the room. The lector reads a phrase, and everybody in the room writes it down. Then he reads another phrase. This moves copying in the direction of mass production, but it has a liability: What happens when two copyists hear different things? As with errors of sight, when errors of hearing make good sense, the copyist may have no prompt to tell him he needs to make a correction.

Errors of Mind

Sometimes errors have their origin in the mind of the copyist. We should not be surprised to find these because the copyists knew only too well how easy it is to make mistakes. Why should they not try to fix those mistakes if they found them in other copyists' work? The problem was that sometimes in their attempts to help, they actually introduced errors into the tradition.

Here's an example: In the following passage I've left out some words in the Lord's Prayer. See if you can figure out which ones:

> Father, hallowed be thy name. Thy kingdom come. Give us each day our daily bread; and forgive us our sins, for we ourselves forgive every one who is indebted to us; and lead us not into temptation.

If I try this exercise in class, I ask my students to raise their hands when they hear the error, and to hold their hands up until I've finished reading. Here's what happens:

> Father, [*Hands go up: where's "our"? Where's "who art in heaven"?*] hallowed be thy name. Thy kingdom come. [*More hands: Where's "thy will be done on earth as it is in heaven"?*] Give us each day our daily bread; and forgive us our sins [*More hands. Should be "trespasses."*], for we ourselves forgive every one who is indebted to us [*Hands: Should be "as we forgive those who have trespassed against us."*]; and lead us not into temptation. [*Add: "but deliver us from evil, for thine is the kingdom, and the power and the glory forever. Amen."*]

Actually, I didn't play fair with my students. The first version above is exactly right, but comes from Luke 11, rather than the more familiar version in Matthew 6. This discovery is usually news to my students. (Did Jesus teach two versions? Did one of the evangelists get it wrong?)

The sense that something was left out, or that something's wrong, is a trick of memory that leads to an error called *assimilation*. Assimilation is the tendency to make one passage read like its parallel. This is common between the first three Gospels, between Galatians and Romans, and between NT quotations and the OT texts from which the quotations were taken.

There are several other common types of errors of mind:

- Improvements of spelling and grammar
- "Corrections" of previous scribal "errors"
- Theological or liturgical alterations
- Additions of theological complements
- Marginal notes (called *glosses*) sometimes added into the manuscript by mistake

So How then Do We Recover the Text of the Autograph?

The answer to this question is that we gather our information and sort it out using two different paradigms. Then we compare the results of the two studies to see if they agree. Almost always they do – in which case we have a kind of independent corroboration, with each paradigm confirming the results of the other paradigm.

Method #1: Internal Transcriptional Probability

The first paradigm looks only at the variation units, but doesn't ask which manuscripts support each variant. Instead, it tries to reconstruct the process by which mistakes are introduced, and then reverse that process. We call this approach *internal transcriptional probability*.

There are five basic rules of internal transcriptional probability, and each one begins with the phrase, *all else being equal. . . .* (By this we mean, "If everything else is precisely in balance, this is what breaks the tie.")

All else being equal, the shorter reading is preferred.

This criterion is based on the observation that the mss tended to grow over time. There are a number of reasons this might happen, such as assimilation or the incorporation of marginal glosses. Sometimes a copyist who had two mss in front of him would discover that they disagree. Rather than choose wrongly, he might include both options. Suppose one ms reads *Jesus*, a second reads *Lord*, and a third reads *Christ*. It's not difficult to see how a copyist, hoping to preserve the original wording, but not knowing how to determine which that was, would simply combine those readings, so we end up with *Lord Jesus Christ*.

We compensate for this tendency by preferring shorter readings over longer ones.

All else being equal, the more difficult reading is preferred.

Sometimes copyists improved the mss they were working with, polishing the grammar, correcting what appeared to deviate from accepted tradition, and so forth. Their intention here was also good: If this is the word of God, we can surely expect it to contain polished prose. Here too the intention to improve sometimes introduced difficulties into the tradition. Once an improvement is made, it gets repeated in all subsequent copies.

We compensate for this tendency by preferring the more difficult reading.

All else being equal, the least assimilated reading is preferred.

We correct for assimilation. This is quite common and is easily identified and corrected.

All else being equal, the reading that best conforms to the author's regular style is preferred.

This is a little subtle, so let's dwell on it for a moment. In English there are two different ways to spell the word *theater* (or *theatre*). We generally use the spelling that was common in the context in which we grew up, and that spelling becomes our default spelling. We might use the alternative, but we'd have to have a reason to do that. In the same way, Greek has two words for lamb—*arnion* or *amnos*. As far as we can tell, the two words were interchangeable. If a writer usually uses one form, but some ms variation uses the alternate form, that difference tells against it. The

Gospel of John uses *amnos*, and if I find a variant that uses *arnion*, I'm going to discount that variant as less probable.

All else being equal, the reading that best explains the rise of the others is preferred.

This criterion is kind of the gatekeeper. Sometimes if I start with one variant, I can explain where the other variants came from. A famous example is the ending of Mark. Some mss contain a long closing (16:9-20). Other mss just quit after v. 8. This criterion asks its question this way:

- If we start with the shorter ending, can we explain why a copyist might add a longer one? (Yes: The short ending is abrupt and leaves all sorts of questions unanswered.)
- If we start with the longer ending, can we explain why some copyist might delete everything after v. 8? (Nope. To do that is to introduce problems into the reading.)

This kind of thinking is part of the puzzle that ends up suggesting that Mark didn't write vv. 9-20.

Method #2: External Manuscript Probabilities

The second paradigm considers only the quality and distribution of the supporting mss. This consideration weighs two elements which, like internal transcriptional probability, begin with the phrase, *all else being equal. . . .*

All else being equal, the reading that is supported by the most reliable manuscripts is preferred.

Let's go back to our diagram of Luke 10:37. What I've done here is put the most likely reading on top. If you look carefully, you'll notice that some mss appear on top more often than others. This means that these mss tend to be more reliable than the others.

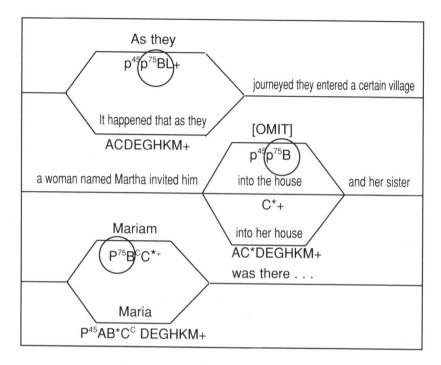

Figure 4.4

If we extended this model through the entire NT, we would have a statistical way of evaluating which mss are more reliable and which are subject to drift. All told, then, with external ms evidence we tend to give these mss greater weight.

All else being equal, the reading that is most distributed through the families is preferred.

This criterion is a little trickier, so we need to linger here for a moment. Remember that errors that don't make sense are easier to catch, and errors that do make sense are harder to catch. For this reason, when a *sensible* error is introduced into the tradition, it tends to be duplicated in all later copies. When a whole bunch of mss share the same error (or groups of errors), it seems reasonable to assume they have a common parent or grandparent farther up the line. (This is a little like DNA testing, looking for common distinctive traits.)

When we look at the mss this way, we see that they tend to cluster into families, which show signs of linear descent, like this:

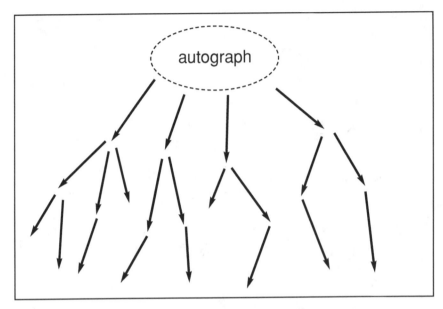

Figure 4.5

The problem with this diagram is that not all mss survived, so we have selective evidence of the families. Even so, the mss fall into four families: *Alexandrian*, *Byzantine*, *Western*, and *Caesarean*. Now, with this criterion, what we're looking for is *wide distribution through the families*.

Suppose the kitchen burned down on my grandparents' farm, and with it went all of Grandma's recipes. My family wants me to reconstruct the original wording of the recipe for apple pie. It was always a family favorite, and copies had been made for the various children and grandchildren over the years; but unfortunately the copies differ from one another, and Grandma's gone and can't tell us which is right. I ask everybody to send me their copies.

First thing I discover: There are some problems with the evidence. Almost all of the copies have *cinnamon*. My brother Joel doesn't have his copy anymore, but his wife Karen made copies for their sons, Adam and Andy. Both of those copies have *cinnamon*, so it's a reasonable guess that Joel's had *cinnamon* too. The second problem is that at this same place, John's copy reads *nutmeg*.

I could show these facts with a chart.

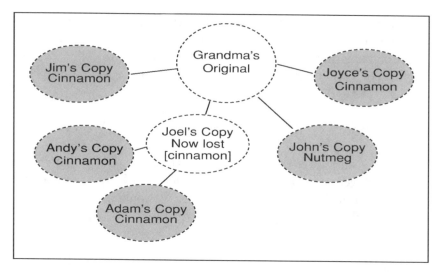

Figure 4.6

In the distribution, how many votes do Andy and Adam get? Only one, since they're only indirect evidence of Joel's one copy. If we were taking a vote, we'd get three to one in favor of *cinnamon*.

Now it happens that John had this huge block party where he and his wife DiAnn served up generous slices of Grandma's apple pie. Everybody under the sun wanted a copy of the recipe. It also happens that John is a printer, so he trotted down to his shop and ran off 5,000 copies (it was a really big party). This changes the diagram:

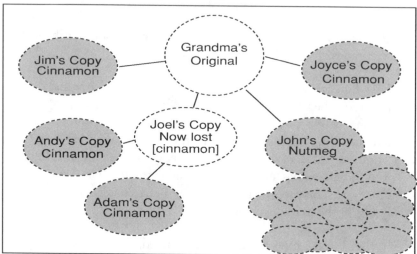

Figure 4.7

How many votes do the 5,000 copies get? Only one, for exactly the same reason Adam and Andy only got one vote: They're indirect evidence of John's single copy. As I make my decision about Grandma's autograph, I don't give them that much weight. Instead, I look for distribution through the families.

So How Do We Know the Autographs Are Lost?

Now we can answer this question. Say we make a Claremont Profile diagram of every verse in one of the books in the NT, and say we always put the most likely reading on the top line. We could reasonably expect the autograph of that book would meet two criteria:

- First, the siglum of the autograph would always appear on the top line.
- Second, that manuscript would contain only that one book and no others.

None of the mss we have meets both of these two criteria, so it's reasonable to conclude that the autographs are lost.

Eclecticism: Working the Internal and External Evidence Together

But the fact that the autographs are lost doesn't mean that the *texts* of the autographs are lost. Here's what we do.

- First, for each variation unit we collect all the evidence and display it on the Claremont Profile grid like we find in figure 4.2.
- Second, we examine the wording to see if we can explain the differences using the tools of internal transcriptional probability.
- Third, we check to see which mss support each reading and how well those readings are distributed among the four families.
- Finally, we compare the results of the internal evidence with the results of the external evidence.

Surprise! Ninety-nine times of one hundred, the two types of study agree. This equals a form of independent corroboration. When the two internal and external methods reach the same results, we know we've found the *text* of the autograph.

But once in a long while they don't agree. Then we have to sift through everything *for each individual variant* to see if we can't weight them in a more careful way. This is the point at which Textual Criticism turns from science to art. Because the weighting may be slightly different for each variant, this method is called *eclecticism*.

The Debate about the King James Version

Now we're in a position to understand the debate about the King James Version, which is really a debate about method. Not everybody agrees that eclecticism is the right way to go about doing Textual Criticism.

The KJV was translated in 1611, from what's called the *Received Text* (Latin: *Textus Receptus*; abbreviation: TR). But the TR is based on the readings of the single family of manuscripts that happens to be the most numerous. In fact, the Byzantine family contains more mss than all the other families combined. We could diagram this way:

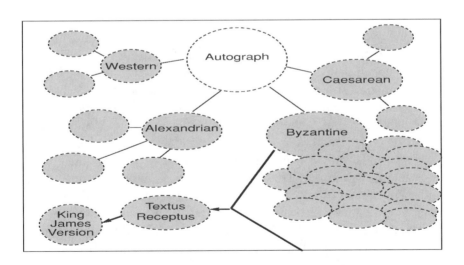

Figure 4.8

The problem is, how do we explain this diagram? Advocates of the KJV explain it one way, and the eclectics explain it another way.

Advocates of the KJV

The advocates of the KJV argued that the best explanation for the large quantity of Byzantine mss is that this is the oldest tradition. Their reasoning is simple: The earlier the father, the greater the number of descendants. According to this view, the other families have relatively fewer descendants because they were recognized as defective and so weren't copied as frequently, or were even discarded completely. For this reason, advocates of the KJV discount the considerations of internal transcriptional probability, and they read the external manuscript evidence using only one criterion:

All else being equal, the reading that is supported by
the majority of the mss is preferred.

This means dropping all that stuff about transcriptional probability, quality of mss, and distribution through the families. To be fair, advocates of this view should really be called advocates of the majority text. The way they see it, the connection with the King James Version is secondary and unimportant.

Opponents of the KJV

In answer to the advocates of the majority text, the eclectics ask this question: If the families all derive from the Byzantine Recension, how does it happen that they sometimes share readings *against* their parent?

The eclectics also have a completely different explanation for the large number of mss in the Byzantine family. By the fourth century, they say, Greek was becoming less and less well known in the Mediterranean basin. As Greek gave way to Latin, fewer and fewer people were able to copy mss, and eventually the copying became a kind of centralized industry, based in Byzantium. The copyists at Byzantium happened to follow the opposite rules from the ones we discussed above. When their exemplars differed, they added the readings together. When there were divine names, they piled them up. When the Gospels differed from each other, they "corrected" the differences by assimilation. The result was the Byzantine Recension.

The greater number of Byzantine mss can be explained this way: Copies were made in Byzantium, and then carried throughout the empire, where they became the parents of other copies, which became the parents of other copies, until eventually the Byzantine Recension dominated the field. When the printing press was invented, it seemed natural to rely on the wording of the Byzantine Recension, which gave us the TR. The TR was the basis of the KJV.

And in the Pews . . .

Here's where historical study and devotional practice come to conflict: When people in the pews compare the newer translations with the wording of the KJV, it sometimes feels like somebody has been trying to damage the Bible. Remember the five rules of internal transcriptional probability?

All else being equal . . .

- *The shorter reading is preferred.*
- *The more difficult reading is preferred.*
- *The least assimilated reading is preferred.*
- *The reading that best conforms to author's regular style is preferred.*
- *The reading that best explains the rise of the others is preferred.*

When people compared the new translations with the KJV, what they discovered was that the stories were sometimes shorter, or more difficult, or there were greater differences among the Gospels. In the KJV, the Lord's Prayer in Luke reads just like the Lord's Prayer in Matthew, and if people were used to that, the shorter prayer in the newer translations naturally felt odd. It *felt* like somebody had taken something away. Sometimes the divine names were reduced from two or three to one; *Lord Jesus Christ* might be shortened to just *Jesus*. It *felt* like somebody was messing with Scripture, taking out some of the buttresses of the faith. To a lot of people, it looked—or rather *felt*—like some godless rascals were up to no good.

Let's remember (from chapter 3) that *feeling* isn't a very good measure of validity; we need sterner stuff than that.

Almost all trained text critics agree that the eclectic approach provides the best accounting for the evidence. A small but vocal minority are advocates of the KJV. Whichever method we endorse, it's important that we remember that this is an historical problem that has to be resolved with precise, accurate information and careful thought. We can't decide this issue based solely on what feels right because something may feel right just because we're used to it, rather than because it makes good rational sense.

But Isn't This the Word of God?

Sometimes when I tell students at the university about the variations in the mss, there's a general panic: Isn't this the Word of God? I remember one young student who objected with special passion: "But, Professor, if there are mistakes in the copies, then *God cannot be <u>God</u>!*" (Literally, he said this.)

My response is threefold: First, these are cold, hard, observable facts. One can only ignore them as an act of moral blindness.

Second, almost all churches that have a statement on the inerrancy of Scripture qualify that statement very carefully: The Scriptures are inerrant in the *text of the autographs*. No claim of inerrancy is made for the history of copying. One of the most influential statements on biblical inerrancy is known as the Chicago Statement. Here's what the Chicago Statement says about the manuscripts:

> *Article* X: We affirm that inspiration, strictly speaking, *applies only to the autographic text of Scripture*, which in the providence of God can be ascertained from available manuscripts with great accuracy. We further affirm that copies and translations of Scripture are the Word of God to the extent that they faithfully represent the original.
>
> We deny that any essential element of the Christian faith is affected by the absence of the autographs. We further deny that this absence renders the assertion of Biblical inerrancy invalid or irrelevant.

Third, although this problem is hard, it's not unsolvable. I began by noting that there are somewhere in the vicinity of 300,000 manuscript variations. The text critics have resolved all but about 50, and *no point of doctrine rests on a disputed text.*

So things aren't as bad as they appear. We can do this. It's hard, but it's possible. Let's close this chapter with a word from a well-known biblical scholar named Larry Hurtado:

> The Christian who regards the Bible as the Word of God at the same time recognizes that this Word was transmitted through time by human agents who, though they were not always perfect in their work, have

placed all subsequent students of the Bible in their debt. We are in no position to complain about their work, for we are wholly dependent upon them for any direct contact with the biblical documents, and we owe them gratitude for their labors.[1]

So How Do I Find Out More about This Topic?

For a good introduction to the whole history of this discussion, see Bruce Metzger and Bart D. Ehrman, *The Text of the New Testament: Its Transmission, Corruption, and Restoration* (4th edn.: Oxford: Oxford University Press, 2005). For commentary on individual variants, see Bruce Metzger, A *Textual Commentary on the Greek New Testament* (New York: United Bible Societies, 1971).

For both sides of the debate about the KJV, you might want to compare: Gordon Fee, "Modern Textual Criticism and the Revival of the *Textus Receptus*," *Journal of the Evangelical Theological Society* 21 (1978): 19-33. Zane Hodges, "Modern Textual Criticism and the Majority Text," *Journal of the Evangelical Theological Society* 21 (1978): 143-55. Hodges advocates for the majority text; Fee opposes it.

Chapter 5

YOUR VERSION, MY VERSION

Thinking about Translation Theory

Our work with textual criticism gave us a way to reconstruct the wording of the autographs. If this were a class at the university, I would tell you that the next step is to make a preliminary translation. But it's not a class, so I'll modify the prompt: pick out a good translation to use as a basis for your research. But how do we do that?

Sometime around 180 BC, a prominent Jewish scholar named ben Sirach made a collection of wise sayings. These were originally written in Hebrew, but were later translated into Greek by ben Sirach's grandson. The grandson attached the following little comment to the beginning of his work:

> You are therefore entreated to undertake the reading of this book with kindliness and attentiveness and to be indulgent if in any parts of what we have labored to interpret we seem to fall short in the rendering of some phrases. *For when things spoken in Hebrew are translated into another language they have not quite the same meaning. And not only these things which follow, but the law itself, and the prophecies and the rest of the books convey a different meaning when spoken in their original language.*

In a nutshell, that's the problem of translation: Things "convey a different meaning when spoken in their original language."

Preliminary Terms

How do we solve that problem? Let's begin with some definitions of terms.

Version

In biblical scholarship, we use the term *version* as an exact synonym for the term *translation*.

Original (or Source) Language

By this we mean the language out of which the translation is made. The source language for NT translation is Koine Greek, which we'll discuss in chapter 6.

Receptor (or Target) Language

This refers to the language into which the translation is made.

Using these terms, let's rephrase ben Sirach's grandson's opening quote:

> For when things spoken in a *source language* are translated into a *receptor language*, they have not quite the same meaning. And not only these things that follow, but the law itself, and the prophecies and the rest of the books convey a different meaning when spoken in their *source language*.

Theory of Translation

Why does something "convey a different meaning" when translated into a different language? There are lots of contributing factors. Here we'll just mention five. Others will become clear in later chapters of this book.

First, *vocabularies don't overlap exactly*. Eskimos have more than fifty words for snow. In English, I can think of maybe five—flurry, precipitation, snow. (OK three.) Some languages have words that are entirely lacking in other languages. Imagine you live in the nineteenth century, and you're asked to translate John 10:27 for a village of Eskimos: "My sheep know my voice." Since Eskimos don't have sheep, you'd need to find the closest cultural parallel; so you might come up with this: "My huskies know my voice."

The Amahuaca Indians in the Amazon basin don't have wolves, so Wycliffe translator Robert Russell rendered John 10:12 this way:

> The good shepherd lays down his life for the sheep, but the hireling, when he sees the tiger coming, flees, because the sheep are not his.

Notice that Russell had to interpret this passage on the way to his translation. He determined what particular details are important in the source language—the threat wolves pose to shepherds—and he had to find a culturally comparable relationship in the target language. When he did this, he made a change in the details in order to be true to the point.

Second, *connotations in one language are not automatically paralleled in another language*. For example, in some parts of Mexico, bread is a second-rate food. You only eat bread when you're out of tortillas. It makes sense, then, to translate John 6:35 this way: "I am the tortilla of life."

Third, *grammatical structures don't overlap exactly*. In the same way that words have different ranges of meaning, grammatical relationships also differ from language to language. For example, in English, the function of a word in a sentence is indicated by word order. ("Michal Beth kissed John," means something altogether different from "John kissed Michal Beth," even though the two sentences have the same words.) In Greek, grammatical function is indicated by a change of spelling. That means a Greek sentence can throw something to the front to create emphasis, but without changing the grammatical relationships between the words.

One problem with grammar has recently become a matter of debate among translators: The Greek language uses the masculine gender as the inclusive gender. Say you have 100 people in a room—99 women, 1 man. Greek describes the group with the masculine gender. Unless translators factor that linguistic habit into their translations, their readers will think the group is all men; and that in turn may seriously distort their understanding of the role of women in early Christianity.

A fourth problem faced by translators has to do with idioms and euphemisms. All languages have phrases that function like words, or peculiar ways of saying something that could not be deduced from the parts. These are called idioms. (A good example is, "Hard? Naw. It'll be a piece of cake.") A euphemism is an idiom that allows us to say something objectionable in a more polite way. "She passed away," is a euphemism. "He croaked," is an idiom.

Finally, translators have to decide what to do about *weights, measures,* and *units of money.* How do you translate *cubit, span, ephah?* How much is a *denarius?* How much is a *widow's mite?* If you translate into modern units like dollars and cents, your translation may make sense to Americans, but leave the British readers puzzled. What about the rest of the world? And it won't be very long before inflation makes your translation into mis-translation.

The upshot of these difficulties is that translators have to make decisions about how close they want to stay to the idioms and diction of the source language and how far they want to accommodate the idioms and diction of the receptor language. If you stay really close to the source, the translation sounds awkward and foreign in the reader's ears. On the other hand, the more you accommodate the receptor language, the more you have to leave the source language behind.

Here's a transcription of an interview between the Hungarian journal *Blikk* and the American actress, "Material Girl," and sometime mystic, Madonna. The questions were asked first in Hungarian, then translated into English. Madonna's English answers were translated back into Hungarian. Then the whole thing was translated back into English. (Forgive me, but I've toned it down a notch. This book is a family show.)

> Blikk: Madonna, Budapest says hello with arms that are spread-eagled. Did you have a visit here that was agreeable? Are you in good odor? You are the biggest fan of our young people who hear your musical productions and like to move their bodies in response.

> Madonna: Thank you for saying these compliments (holds up hands).

> Blikk: Madonna, let's cut toward the hunt. Are you a bold hussy-woman that feasts on men who are tops?

> Madonna: Yes, yes, this is certainly something that brings to the surface my longings. In America it is not considered to be mentally ill when a woman advances on her prey in a discotheque setting with hearty cocktails present.

> Blikk: Is this how you met Carlos? Did you know he was heaven-sent right off the stick?

Madonna: But as regards those questions, enough! I am a
woman and not a test-mouse! Carlos is an everyday person who
is in the orbit of a star who is being muscle-trained by him.

Blikk: Thank you for your candid chitchat.

Madonna: No problem, friend who is a girl.[1]

Translators of the Bible also have to worry about coming off wooden
like that. Once Billy Graham was preaching in Russia on the passage from
Paul that says, "The body is weak, but the spirit is strong." The translator,
trying hard to get at a good, close rendering, said something that came
out as, "He can't stand up, but he has good vodka."

Working across the Spectrum

What this means is that we could set up a spectrum of translations,
with *wooden*, awkward translations on the far right, and looser *paraphrases* on the far left. In the middle we'll place what are called *dynamic
equivalency* (or sometimes *functional equivalency*). The best way to show
this movement is with an example, for which I've chosen a section of
Romans 7.

Wooden Translations

Wooden translations try to stay close to the original in both diction
and facts. The hallmark of a good wooden translation is *re-translatability*. When we aim for re-translatability, we're saying something like, "If
I translated this back into Greek, would I get the same Greek?" That
means translating verbs with verbs, nouns with nouns, adjectives with
adjectives. Idiomatic phrases are rendered literally, rather than being
transformed lock-stock-and-barrel into fresh idioms in the receptor
language.

King James Version and New King James Version
In chapter 4 we saw already that the biggest difference between the
KJV (and NKJV) and the other translations is that they're based on
different reconstructions of the underlying Greek text. In terms of their

actual translation style, these two versions are quite wooden. (The NKJV is based on the same textual principles as the original KJV—majority text only—but has updated the vocabulary to take into account changes in the English language since 1611.) Here's Romans 7:14-20 from the KJV:

> For we know that the law is spiritual: but I am carnal, sold under sin. For that which I do I allow not: for what I would, that do I not; but what I hate, that do I. If then I do that which I would not, I consent unto the law that it is good. Now then it is no more I that do it, but sin that dwelleth in me. For I know that in me (that is, in my flesh,) dwelleth no good thing: for to will is present with me; but how to perform that which is good I find not. For the good that I would I do not: but the evil which I would not, that I do. Now if I do that I would not, it is no more I that do it, but sin that dwelleth in me.

New American Standard Bible

Another wooden translation is the *New American Standard Bible*. This is an update of the 1901 American Standard Version published by the Lockman Foundation.

> For we know that the Law is spiritual, but I am of flesh, sold into bondage to sin. For what I am doing, I do not understand; for I am not practicing what I would like to do, but I am doing the very thing I hate. But if I do the very thing I do not want to do, I agree with the Law, confessing that the Law is good. So now, no longer am I the one doing it, but sin which dwells in me. For I know that nothing good dwells in me, that is, in my flesh; for the willing is present in me, but the doing of the good is not. For the good that I want, I do not do, but I practice the very evil that I do not want. But if I am doing the very thing I do not want, I am no longer the one doing it, but sin which dwells in me.

Functional Equivalency Translations

Functional equivalency translations cut a deal with the receptor language. Instead of translating word-for-word, they tend to translate concept-for-concept. They're willing to adapt to the receptor language in matters of style and idiom, but they try to stay close to the source language in matters of cultural practices and historical fact. The objective of functional equivalency translations is to have the same impact on the receptor audience as the original had in Greek, but without compromising matters of historical fact. (For this reason, these are also sometimes called Dynamic Equivalency translations.)

The Revised Standard Version

A good example of a functional equivalency translation is the *Revised Standard Version of the Bible*:

> We know that the law is spiritual; but I am carnal, sold under sin. I do not understand my own actions. For I do not do what I want, but I do the very thing I hate. Now if I do what I do not want, I agree that the law is good. So then it is no longer I that do it, but sin which dwells within me. For I know that nothing good dwells within me, that is, in my flesh. I can will what is right, but I cannot do it.

The New Revised Standard Version

The *New Revised Standard Version of the Bible* is an update of the RSV, with this difference: It makes a conscious effort toward gender equity in translation. For example, in Romans 16:7 Paul greets Andronicus and Junias. The RSV translates this way:

> Greet Andronicus and Junias, my *kinsmen* and my fellow prisoners; they are *men of note* among the apostles, and they were in Christ before me.

But because Greek uses the masculine gender, it's not at all clear that Junias was male. In fact, there seems to be very little attestation for this name used for a man before about AD 500. The NRSV makes an adjustment to allow for the possibility that Junias was really a woman, Junia:

> Greet Andronicus and Junia, my *relatives* who were in prison with me; they are *prominent* among the apostles, and they were in Christ before I was.

Generally speaking, the NRSV is the translation of choice among professional biblical scholars.

New International Version and Today's New International Version

The translation of choice in Evangelical churches seems to be the *New International Version*, and—more recently—its daughter, *Today's New International Version*. These are both functional equivalency translations. The following is from the TNIV:

We know that the law is spiritual; but I am unspiritual, sold as a slave to sin. I do not understand what I do. For what I want to do I do not do, but what I hate I do. And if I do what I do not want to do, I agree that the law is good. As it is, it is no longer I myself who do it, but it is sin living in me. I know that good itself does not dwell in me, that is, in my sinful nature. For I have the desire to do what is good, but I cannot carry it out. For I do not do the good I want to do, but the evil I do not want to do—this I keep on doing. Now if I do what I do not want to do, it is no longer I who do it, but it is sin living in me that does it.

Paraphrases

Paraphrases throw up their hands and come into the receptor language in both diction and facts. For example, in Luke 10:4, Jesus tells the disciples to take nothing for their missionary journey: "carry no purse, no bag, no sandals . . ." (RSV). Eugene Petersen's paraphrase, *The Message*, reads this way: "Travel light. Comb and toothbrush and no extra luggage."

So paraphrases can take liberties, which drives some scholars and pastors nuts. I think they have their place. Sometimes they can be quite perceptive. Here's how Kenneth Taylor renders Romans 7:16: "I know perfectly well that what I am doing is wrong, and *my bad conscience proves that I agree with these laws I am breaking.*" I find that refreshingly clear.

The Message

Probably the best-known paraphrase in use today is *The Message* by Eugene Petersen. Here's *The Message* on Romans 7:

> But I need something *more!* For if I know the law but still can't keep it, and if the power of sin within me keeps sabotaging my best intentions, I obviously need help! I realize that I don't have what it takes. I can will it, but I can't *do* it. I decide to do good, but then I don't *really* do it; I decide not to do bad, but then I do it anyway . . .

Letters to Street Christians

My favorite paraphrase is *Letters to Street Christians*, left over from the 1960s. The translation committee is identified simply as, "two brothers from Berkeley." Same passage from Romans 7:

When I first met Jesus I was alive with his Spirit, and didn't even think about the law. But then it started laying its trips on me again, and I got sick and wasted in my life with Jesus. The law which was supposed to point me to life was killing me. My old self grabbed God's good law, faked me out, and killed my walk with Jesus.

What Difference Does This Make?

Let's go back now and see how much drift we have. Suppose we compare our passage in the KJV with the same passage in *Letters to Street Christians*:

King James Version	Letters to Street Christians
And the commandment,	The law
which was ordained to life,	which was supposed to point me to life
I found to be unto death;	was killing me.
for sin, taking occasion	My old self grabbed
by the commandment,	God's good law,
deceived me	faked me out,
and by it slew me.	and killed my walk with Jesus.

Which Is Best?

Inevitably somebody asks which is best, but that's not the best way to put the question. A better way is to ask which is best *for which purposes*.

For rapid reading. Suppose you want to slip into the biblical story the way you would a novel, with easy access to the flow of movement. If that's what you want, stay clear of the wooden translations. They'll trip you up. Try reading the paraphrases.

For detailed study, go the other direction.

For witnessing, everything depends on who you're talking to. Say you're talking to someone from the Church of Jesus Christ of the Latter Day Saints (aka The Mormons). Mormons prefer the KJV. It's best to stick with that. But there are street people out there who left the church because they think that maybe God only speaks King James English. (Does God "get" rap?) Why not try out a paraphrase?

For worship, it may be best to stay with the functional equivalency translations. These are easy to read and hear; and because they're careful with diction, they often have a pleasing, balanced sound for reading out loud in church.

Whatever translation you choose, remember that there's a difference between what something *says* and what it *means*. We still have a journey ahead. In chapter 6, we set out the roadmap of that journey.

PART II

THE HOW OF EXEGESIS

Once we've reconstructed the wording of the original and made (or adopted) a preliminary translation, we're ready to think about getting from what the text *says* to what it *meant*. The next few chapters set out the theories of the various disciplines and subdisciplines necessary to do that.

As you read this stuff, you'll notice right away that what we're doing is shifting from paradigm to paradigm. This is like trading hats as we move from word study to context study to study of form. Each paradigm tells us some things but overlooks others.

Some students find the array of paradigms a little confusing. Here are a couple of ways to think about that, to keep everything under control. The first is to have a single overarching paradigm in which the parts all fit together. That's what we do in chapter 6, which I call "The Master Paradigm." As you learn the other paradigms, you can keep coming back to the Master Paradigm to see where the connections are. Then in chapters 7–16, we'll set out the various parts of that paradigm. The important thing is to learn each part, then practice noticing how the parts fit together. We'll look at an example in chapter 17.

A second way to deal with the variety of paradigms is to think of them as sets of skills that are sometimes needed and sometimes not. Imagine yourself learning to play piano. You spend twenty minutes practicing your scales, and then twenty minutes getting the meter right, and twenty minutes practicing on some song. Each of these is an essential part of learning to play piano, and you may have to practice 'til your fingers hurt. That's the only way to get to the place where they do what they have to do automatically. Now imagine that one day you pick up some sheet music and begin to play. You tickle the keys, and what comes out of the piano makes your mother cry. Every score has its own combination of notes; each score is different, and successful piano playing consists of having the proper range of skills, *combined with* the ability to know when to use each skill.

If this example doesn't work for you, try changing out the imagery to tennis or golf or driving a car. The point is that once you know the skills, you can "play" them as you need them. At first it's work, but pretty soon a kind of muscle memory kicks in, and you find yourself just diving in and playing, losing yourself in the music (or game or street or whatever). In the same way, the exegesis of each passage of Scripture will call on you to use some combination of skills, but no two passages will test your skills in exactly the same ways.

If you practice noticing how the paradigms work together, pretty soon the reactions become second nature, and the confusion clears up.

Chapter 6

THE MASTER PARADIGM

An Introduction to Exegesis

Exegesis \ek-suh-JEE-sis\, *noun; plural: exegeses* \-seez\: *Exposition; explanation; especially, a critical explanation of a text.*

The following story is true. The names have been changed to protect the innocent. My parents (we'll call them Kathleen and Harry) were divorced when I was twelve years old. Who knows why? One contributing factor I know about had to do with a letter my mother wrote.

For as long as I can remember, my father was active in the local Boy Scouts organization. For a time he was scoutmaster to a troop of Scouts who were developmentally disabled—with these boys he was a model of patience, a genuine and thoughtful caregiver.

One day my mother received a note in the mail from one of the other scoutmasters, whom I'll call James Cook. (Not his real name. If you know a James Cook, this is not the guy.) It seems that my father was going to be given an award for his work, and that the award was going to be a surprise during the annual awards banquet. The presenter would say, "The recipient of this year's Breakthrough to Youth award was born in Perry, Oklahoma, ..." and then they would tell his life story. The fact that the recipient was my father would gradually dawn on him as the

71

announcement unfolded. Mr. Cook wanted to know when he could meet with my mother to learn my father's story.

My mother wrote back the following note:

Dear James—
Come over on Thursday afternoon. Harry will still be at work, the children will be at school, we'll have the whole afternoon to ourselves uninterrupted.

—Kathleen

She put the note in the outgoing mail, where my father found it. When he read it, he supplied all the wrong background information. That's the snowball that eventually avalanched into my parents' divorce.

I've included this story here for several reasons. The obvious point is that there was a right way to read Mr. Cook's note. My father read it the wrong way, and it cost him his marriage. (More precisely, he *exegeted* it the wrong way.) The inescapable, nonnegotiable, take-it-to-the-bank point is that we're not free to draw whatever conclusions we want just because they may make sense to us. The less obvious point is that in order to grasp the more obvious point, you have to think about my illustration in particular ways. You have to bring certain kinds of outside information to the reading.

In this chapter we overview the basic steps involved in getting it right. Authors expect readers to follow certain rules, and those rules require the reader to supply a certain set of facts as background. Sometimes those facts are quite precise and detailed. My mother's note presupposes certain very specific information she and James shared, but which my father didn't know. Lacking that specific information, my father supplied the wrong background and so defaulted to the only other explanation he could think of.

Remember our definition of *exegesis* from chapter 2? We said that *exegesis* is the systematic recovery of the meaning of the text in its original context, the "there and then." Here let's refine that a bit, since "meaning" has to do with *intention* (on the part of the author) and *understanding* (on the part of the reader): *Exegesis* is the systematic recovery of the meaning the author intended. What we're trying to do here is get from what is *said* to what is *meant*.

In order to do that, we need to design a paradigm that replicates the activities the authors of the Bible expected their readers would engage in.

It would replicate the *prior information* the original readers were expected to have in hand; it would understand the biases and commitments (or *predispositions*) of the original reader; it would respect the *protocols*, or reading conventions, for which the text was designed, and it would respect the assumptions about reality (or *presuppositions*) the writers expected their readers would bring with them to the reading.

The Greek of the NT Is Ordinary Language

The reason we can even do exegesis is that the Greek of the NT is ordinary language, rather than magical or mystical language. If the Bible were written in some supernatural language, historical study wouldn't do us any good. The repertoire of cultural knowledge wouldn't matter, either. We'd have to find some magic glasses with supernatural lenses like the ones the Latter Day Saints say Joseph Smith used to translate the Book of Mormon from "Reformed Egyptian."

Holy Spirit Greek?

It wasn't always clear that NT Greek was ordinary language. For a long time, people thought it was a special kind of Greek, which they called *Holy Spirit Greek*. They based this conclusion on what seemed like good evidence at the time. Suppose we made a list of all the different vocabulary words found in the Greek NT. The list would contain somewhere around 5,600 words. About 10 percent of those words are not found anywhere in the polished Greek of the classical authors. How to explain that? One explanation that seemed to make sense was that the NT was written in a special dialect inspired especially for the NT writers by the Holy Spirit—Holy Spirit Greek.

That may sound a little odd to us today, but theologians in the nineteenth century found it attractive for two reasons. First, this seemed to fit into a viewpoint that said that the best competence for reading the Bible was to be a spiritual person and that the unregenerate person was automatically disqualified. Second, they found it helpful in setting up one of their most important theological ideas: The interpretation of the Bible calls for a "special hermeneutic," and therefore methods of interpretation that worked for other kinds of ancient literature were inappropriate for the Bible. In that way, they could resist the historians who wanted to interpret the Bible using the same tools they used with other ancient texts.

Koine Greek Instead!

Then at the turn of the twentieth century, scholars discovered that most of the missing vocabulary words are found in the trash-dump of history—receipts, bills of lading, letters written home by lonely sailors—the sort of things we write down, read once, then throw away. This discovery told us that the Greek of the NT was not so much Holy Spirit Greek as it was ordinary street Greek, the Greek of the *koine*, or common people. The missing vocabulary words were the sorts of words that never make it into polished, literary prose, so they were missing from the Greek classics.

The Principle of Accommodation

The idea that the Greek of the NT is ordinary language gives rise to a concept theologians call the *principle of accommodation*. This principle says that since we couldn't understand God on God's terms, God spoke to us in our own.

When my children were little, we experienced an earthquake in the middle of the night. All three came running into our bedroom, frightened and confused. "Daddy, what's happening?" I did *not* say to them, "A minor movement of the earth's tectonic plates, kids. We're 15.4 miles from the San Andreas fault." I said something more like, "The ground wiggled." I had *accommodated* myself to their vocabulary. This is what God has done for us. He speaks to us in human terms. No doubt much of the mystery of life would be cleared up if we could understand everything on God's terms, but our minds and hearts are limited, and God's are not.

But the principle of accommodation shouldn't be made to mean that the whole truth of the Bible is understandable in baby terms. (Though there may be good warrant for such a view: Someone once remarked that the Gospel of John is a pool in which a child can wade and an elephant can swim.) As my kids grew, I changed my vocabulary and table talk to keep pace with their growth. Now that they're adults, they can handle better explanations. If they still needed "The ground wiggled," something would be terribly wrong. The principle of accommodation continues to apply no matter how smart we are because God's ways are always higher still. When someone like Mr. Einstein or Mr. Hawking contemplates the heavens, when the extraordinary order and complexity of the universe boggles their brilliant brains, even then, God is higher still.

There turns out to be a hidden benefit to this discovery that the Bible was written in ordinary language: We already know a lot about how to read it: Because Greek is ordinary language, we should use the same kinds of strategies to decode that we would use with other ordinary language.

Suppose we diagram the process like this:

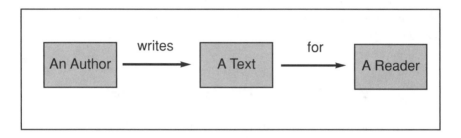

Figure 6.1

Authorial Intention

My story of my mother's letter to Mr. Cook illustrates an important principle, a principle where most conservative interpreters come down: The primary thing to keep in mind when doing exegesis is *author's intention*. Just imagine my mom's response to my father when she found out he had read her note to Mr. Cook: "That's not what I meant." But if the meaning of words rests in whatever the reader chooses to make of them, my mother's reaction would be nonsensical. The very claim, "that's not what I meant" rests upon the assumption that speakers are in charge of the meaning of what they say.

The Authorial Reader

My mother's letter also helps us clarify what we mean by the word *reader*. In this book, when we use the term *reader* we mean, "the reader that the author had in mind as he wrote." NT scholars call such a reader the *authorial reader*. (My mother's *authorial reader* was Mr. Cook; it was not my father.)

The Literary Repertoire

The authorial reader is expected to have in hand a specific repertoire of background information. Mr. Cook knew stuff my father didn't know. I call that background information the *literary repertoire*. Simply put, if we supply the wrong literary repertoire, we will automatically misread.

The challenge, then, is to reconstruct the repertoire of the authorial reader and then ask carefully how that reader was expected to use that repertoire to determine the meaning of the text. This, in short, is exegesis.

A Short Course on Language

But how do we do that? This is the question we address in the remainder of this chapter: Recognizing that the Greek of the NT is ordinary language, is it possible to construct a paradigm that will duplicate what the writers of the Bible expected their authorial readers to do with their texts? Remembering that paradigms consist of four parts enables us to refine the question this way: Can we build a paradigm that recreates the presuppositions, predispositions, prior information, and protocols the ancient reader would have used? I believe we can, precisely because ordinary language has certain properties that are consistent regardless of culture. This means we're already half-way home. We already know a lot about what to do when we read the Bible.

In the remainder of this chapter, we'll have a short discussion about how language works. Then in the following chapters we'll adapt this model to fit the kinds of special challenges we face when we read an ancient document like the Bible.

There are four primary characteristics of language:

- *Language is selective.* It can't say everything, but has to leave some things out.
- *Language is inherently ambiguous.* Because words must sometimes carry double meanings, language is potentially ambiguous.
- *Language is polyvalent.* By this we mean that it carries meaning on a variety of levels—emotional, cognitive, social, and personal.
- *Language is linear.* It can only present its information in a specific sequence, one word after another.

These are features of language *as such*, and therefore of objective, historical, or scientific language as well as imaginative and figurative language. They're features of English, but also of Chinese. The problems created by these features are overcome in various ways by various types of writing. For example, scientific language—like a paper published in the *Journal of the American Medical Association*—has to pare away ambiguities by using a rigidly precise technical vocabulary and by defining context in terms of standardized forms and commonly recognized scientific procedures. By contrast, literary language—like poetry—tends to *use* ambiguity to force the reader into fresh perspectives.

So scientific language deals with the features of language in one way, while poetical language deals with them in another. Yet for both, the primary features are central organizing concerns. Since these are native to language as such, it's worth looking at them more closely.

Language Is Selective

My father misread my mother's letter to Mr. Cook because he supplied the wrong background information. This introduces us to the first primary feature of language: *Language is selective*. It has to be this way. If we don't leave something out, the language becomes too cumbersome. For this reason, all texts require their readers to fill in gaps by drawing on a specific repertoire of background facts.

We can examine gap-filling using the strategies of cognitive science. In 1971, D. R. Dooling and R. Lachman tested comprehension and recall for paragraphs such as the following:

> With hocked gems financing him, our hero bravely defied all scornful laughter that tried to prevent his scheme. Your eyes deceive you, he had said, an egg not a table correctly typifies this unexplored planet. Now three sisters sought proof, forging along sometimes through calm[?] vastness, yet more often over turbulent peaks and valleys. Days became weeks as many doubters spread fearful rumours about the edge. At last, from nowhere, welcome winged creatures appeared, signifying momentous success.[1]

A second group heard the same paragraph, only with a title: "Columbus Discovers America." Now read the paragraph again.

Test results showed a dramatic increase in comprehension and recall. (If you don't believe me, try reading this paragraph to a friend, first without the title, then with it. Ninety percent of the time, your friend will respond with, "Ah!") What this experiment shows is that we absolutely have to understand the repertoire of background facts the writers assumed their readers would already know, and what they therefore don't supply. This also shows, albeit indirectly, that if we fill in the gaps with a wrong set of background facts, we can hardly help but draw conclusions that the writer would not have intended.

This activity of gap-filling goes on all the time, whenever we communicate. Consider the gap-filling in the following short *deep thought*, by Jack Handey:

- I found a skull in the woods, and naturally I called the police. As I waited, I got to thinking about this person—who he was, how he had died, and why did he have deer horns?

When we study the NT, the problem of the gaps is complicated by our natural tendency to fill in the gaps with twenty-first century information, while the authors of the Bible expected their readers to fill in the gaps with first century information. This is like my dad reading my mom's letter against *his* repertoire of information, rather than Mr. Cook's. The important thing to notice here is that we're not free to fill in gaps however we please; we have to do that in a way that's consistent with what the author expected the authorial reader to do.

So this is the first step in valid exegesis: Fill in the gaps by reconstructing the literary repertoire the writer assumed the reader would bring to the reading.

The protocols by which we fill in gaps will occupy our attention in chapters 7–12.

Language Is Inherently Ambiguous

The second primary feature of language derives from the fact that language falls on the ear-gate and not the eye-gate. It's composed primarily of sound. Because the stock of sounds in any given language is necessarily limited, words have to do double duty. *Language is therefore inherently ambiguous.* Richard Lederer calls attention to the following slips of the pen by otherwise competent writers of newspaper headlines:[2]

- Men Recommend More Clubs for Wives
- Defendant's Speech Ends in Long Sentence
- Squad Helps Dog Bite Victim

The task of interpretation requires that we have some way of *disambiguating*, sorting through the options and arriving at a clear understanding of the speaker's intended meaning.

Even when we're not sure who the author was, we still disambiguate. Here's a short assignment: Imagine that you're riding along with a friend from ancient Rome when she asks you about a bumper sticker on the car ahead of you:

Toto, I don't think we're in Kansas anymore.

You could translate for her—*Toto, sentio nos in kansate non iam adesse*—but the translation wouldn't tell her what the bumper sticker *means*, only what it *says*. In order to get at what it means, you have to tie the words to a lot of background information. You'd start by telling her the saying is from the film *The Wizard of Oz*. You might tell her who Dorothy was and that Toto was her dog and that in the film, Kansas was depicted as a dreary, unattractive place—it was filmed in black and white—while the land of Oz was filmed in color and was filled with Munchkins, monkeys, and maniacal witches. (Well, one maniacal witch, but you get my point.) You would then tie that back to the context of the bumper sticker and the fact that the car itself is in, say, California or New York or wherever. The result is therefore a kind of commentary that means something like: "This sure is a whacked-out place."

That, in short form, precisely is exegesis. There's nothing mystical or magical about it. It's a simple, straightforward thing to do.

Here are some more headlines that went awry. Think about how much background information is necessary to figure out what they were supposed to mean.

- New Study of Obesity Looks for Larger Test Group
- Iraqi Head Seeks Arms
- Miners Refuse to Work after Death
- Drunk Gets Nine Months in Violin Case
- Something Went Wrong in Jet Crash, Experts Say

What you should note here is the kinds of stuff your brain does as it sorts these things out. This, then, is the second challenge of valid exegesis: Eliminate any interpretive possibilities that the author could *not* have intended.

The protocols by which we disambiguate will occupy our attention in chapter 13.

Language Is Polyvalent

The third primary feature of language is this: *Language is polyvalent.* By this we mean that it strikes us on several levels. The inherent ambiguity of language suggests that several dimensions of stress may operate at the same time. Sometimes authors intend for us to hear more than one meaning, so we end up with puns and wordplays, allusions, ironies, or double entendres. Suppose you saw a bumper sticker on my car that read, "I love Jerry's kids."

- One level of meaning is obvious to anyone who's familiar with American culture: "Jerry's kids" are young people who have muscular dystrophy.
- If you know me even casually, you'd note a wordplay because my first name is Jerry.
- But the saying acquires a third layer of meaning if you learn that one of my college roommates had muscular dystrophy, and that I was profoundly changed by my experience of living with him.

By *polyvalence* we also mean that we use language to accomplish a lot of different effects. It may evoke responses that are purely intellectual or deeply emotional. It may make us angry, may entertain us, may demand that we make changes in the way we go about our business. It may freak us out.

This, then, is the third major challenge of valid exegesis: Identify any intended additional layers of meaning, such as double entendre, wordplay, irony, and literary allusion. In addition, we have to identify the sometimes multilayered rhetorical impact the writer was intending—to convince, to cajole, to correct, to comfort, or any of the other ways language functions beyond merely getting information out of one head and into another.

The protocols by which we recognize and deal with polyvalence will occupy our attention in chapters 14 and 15.

Language Is Linear

The final primary feature of language is this: *Language is linear.* What happens earlier in a text pushes us in certain directions, and that sets us up to hear what comes later in particular ways. If I hear, "*salagadoola mechicka boola* . . . ," it's a sure bet my mind is going to follow with "*bippidi boppidi boo*." This means that the linearity of language is one of the chief gatekeepers of meaning.

This is the fourth primary challenge of valid exegesis: Consider the impact of the sequence of the text as a factor in an unfolding process of gap-filling.

The protocols by which we deal with sequence will occupy our attention in chapters 16 and 17.

Introducing Rhetoric

At first it would seem that the primary features of language are difficulties to be overcome. It's a problem that language is selective, since the gaps in information leave open the possibility that the reader may fill them in wrongly. The linearity of language creates problems for timing. For example, how do you report two events that in real life went on at the same time? In real life, the events come *simultaneously*, while in a story, they have to come one *after* another. So the four primary features of language are problems.

But the problems also create opportunities for writers to strategize the way they present their material. The fact that language is selective is the reason we can tell white lies. I'm leaving the house, already ten minutes late for a meeting with the provost of the university. The telephone rings. When I hear the ring, I experience a momentary relief, then a private inner battle: I now have a 'truthful' way of apologizing for my tardiness. I can say (quite accurately, but also quite deceptively), "Sorry I was late. The phone rang just as I was leaving the house." I know that the provost will make all the necessary connections and draw the quite incorrect conclusion that I am late *because* of the phone call. If the white lie works, I will have masked the full truth. (With my luck, the call is from the provost himself, wanting to know why I'm late! Oh, well.)

The fact that language is linear means I can withhold information to create suspense or lead my reader in some particular direction. Or I can drop important information at an earlier point in order to nudge the readers' responses to later material in certain directions.

Here's a letter that clearly uses sequence as a rhetorical strategy:

Dear Mom and Dad,
   I have so much to tell you. Because of the fire in my room set off by the riots, I experienced temporary lung damage and had to go to the hospital. While I was there, I fell in love with an orderly, and we have moved in together. I dropped out of school when I found out I was pregnant. He got fired because of his drinking, so we're going to move to Alaska where we might get married after the birth of the baby.
   Your loving daughter
P.S. None of that really happened, but I did flunk a chemistry class, and I wanted you to keep it in perspective.[3]

The manner in which the writer organizes the material to invite specific responses on the part of the reader is called the text's rhetoric.

The point here is that we use language for a lot of different reasons, and not just to get information out of one head and into another. Words are wondrously woven into the woof and warp of the way we see the world. We use language to persuade, alienate, confuse, humor, and entertain. Sometimes we use language to bedevil each other into conversion.

Focusing on the Problem of the Gaps

So the first big challenge is to identify the gaps in the text and fill them in properly. Very much depends upon how information is stored, accessed, and deployed within the mind. We turn to that matter in chapter 7.

Postscript

For reasons I do not fully understand, my father never confronted my mother, so she never learned that he had found the note. I was visiting him once, more than twenty years later, and the subject of my parents' divorce came up. To justify his own action, my father pulled the note *out of his wallet*! I have often thought that if he had been a better exegete he could have saved us all a great deal of grief.

Chapter 7

HOW WE FILL IN GAPS

An Introduction to Schemas

L et's open this chapter with some stories that together illustrate the
first and most important thing we have to do if we want to do valid
exegesis. The first story is a British folktale, and is the shortest story
I know:

> A man woke up terrified and reached for the matches so he could light
> a candle—And. The. Matches. Were. Put. Into. His. Hand.

When I first heard this story it sent a chill shivering up and down my
spine. Once I told this story in class, and a student told me a scarier one:

> It seems she was camping alone in Yosemite National Park. When she
> got home and developed the film of her trip, there was a photograph of
> herself, sleeping.

This one sent a shudder down my back. In this chapter we're interested
in the source of the shudder. What happened here? Why did I shudder?
It wasn't just because of something inside the story. Instead, the
shudder came because of some gap-filling work I was asked to do on
my own.

Once Again, the Problem of Gaps

The gap-filling is necessary because of the first major feature of language: Language is selective—it leaves things out. The gaps in language are like the tumblers of a lock; the proper background information is like a key. Here, then, is the first protocol of good exegesis: We have to identify the gaps and fill them in properly.

Notice that the gap-filling we have in mind here isn't the same thing as reconstructing what actually happened. We don't mean that Mark leaves out information, so we pull in that information from Matthew or Luke. What we're interested in is the way Mark (or Matthew or Paul or whoever) would have expected his readers to understand the words he used. The biblical writers used the gaps to manage the reader's understandings, setting the reader up for surprises, rhetorical turns, and insights.

The Literary Repertoire

The problem of the gaps is at the core of exegesis. We get from what is said to what is meant by correlating what is *said* with what is *assumed*. (We will return to this theme shortly.) I call that assumed background knowledge the *literary repertoire*.

All writers expect their readers to bring a repertoire of outside information with them to the reading. Remember my mother's letter to Mr. Cook in chapter 6? My father misread her letter because he plugged the wrong information into the gaps. If we change that repertoire, we change the meaning of the text. Pure and simple. Not negotiable or nuanceable. Authors write texts for readers *within a specific historical and cultural context, and that context supplies crucial background information—the literary repertoire*. This means we have to modify our diagram to specify that communication only works because of shared information.

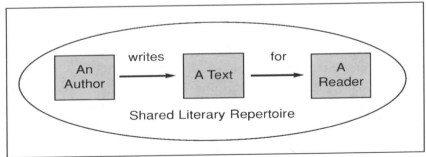

Figure 7.1

That's why the first and most important step in exegesis is to get the literary repertoire right. The next steps have more to do with managing the relationship between the text and the background information the text assumes.

Gap-Filling and the Psychology of Language

But how? How does the mind deal with information that comes packaged up as words? How is it stored? How is it accessed and used? What difficulties do we encounter, and how do we resolve them? We're helped here by discoveries made by cognitive scientists who study the way the brain processes information.

Schemas

We're still learning a lot about this, but even at this stage there appears to be an emerging consensus among the scientists that when we hear a word—for example, *horse*—we don't get a complete set of "horse facts" in our heads. We get a little bit of horse facts. We can go back for more horse facts as we need them. The facts we do get are connected by a kind of web-work. Cognitive scientists use the word *schema* to describe this web-work.

The schemas are what enable us to fill in gaps with appropriate information. For example, Umberto Eco asks what happens when we read the word *princess* in a sentence at the start of a fairy tale:

> If the text says that /once upon a time there was a young princess called Snow White. She was very pretty/, the reader detects by a first semantic analysis of "princess" that Snow White is surely a "woman." The [schema] "princess" is virtually much more complex (for instance, "woman" entails "human female", and a human female should be represented by many properties such as having certain body organs, and so on).[1]

If we were to diagram Eco's comments about the term *princess*, it might look something like this:

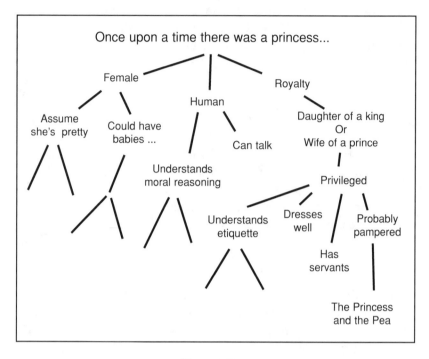

Figure 7.2

Here, then, is a simple and elegant solution to the problem of gaps in language: The basic information for gap-filling is retrieved from the schemas the reader is expected already to have in his or her head. The schemas, in turn, are made up of hierarchies of features, and not complete pictures. As we read along, each word automatically pulls up a range of features, any one of which may later be assumed to be part of the reader's background understanding. Basically, this is just the kind of information we need if we're going to read the Bible the way its authors expected of their original readers.

Schemas Are Not Words, Exactly

Let's sharpen this a little. At first it looks like schemas are words and words are schemas. Each word evokes one schema. But not so. Instead, a single *word* may house several quite different schemas. For example, the word *bug* could mean *insect, infection, listening device, type of automobile, jockey's understudy* (I learned this from a very short student), or *something children do to parents who are trying to write books*. One estimate has it that the 500 most common words in the English language have an average of 28 dictionary meanings each.

The reason this is important for exegesis is that sometimes there's rhetorical play between the different schemas housed under a single word. That's what makes puns and wordplays work, but it's almost always lost in translation. Suppose the headline in the sports section reads:

Mother of Eight Shoots Hole in One

The joke is lost completely when the sentence is translated into, say, French or German. Or say we translate the French tongue-twister:

Le ver vert vire bers le verre vert. Translation: The green worm veers toward the green grass.

Fun French—flat English. What this tells us is that the interplay of synonyms, antonyms, and homonyms is sometimes lost in translation.

Instantiation

When we're actually reading or listening, we can't access whole schemas. Instead, we access them partially. If I asked you to visualize the *supermarket* in which you normally shop, likely you would do so in a large, generalized picture. Now visualize the meat counter and describe the layout of the chicken section. To do that, you have to zoom in to the subschema, *meat counter*. You could zoom in once again to count the rows of chicken packages that are set out. Or you could zoom back to the larger frame of the market as a whole. If you zoom out, however, the *meat counter* part of the schema gets fuzzier.[2] We zoom in and out continually as we read. We access a schema only partially, and then if we need to later, we follow whatever routes are necessary to access and develop additional information connected with that schema.

Context plays an important role in this process. Suppose I said,

The rubber ball shattered when it hit the ground.

This sounds odd because one of the primary features of rubber balls is that they bounce. That's all the information that is accessed. But suppose I said,

After it had been immersed in liquid hydrogen, the rubber ball shattered when it hit the ground.

87

This doesn't sound odd because the reference to liquid hydrogen instantiates additional information about rubber: It gets brittle when exposed to extreme cold. Sometimes inferences drawn from context may be enough to call up secondary information like this, but we have to have clear contextual—or grammatical or formal or thematic or syntactical—evidence to support that conclusion.

The technical term for accessing a schema or part of a schema is *instantiation*.

Schemas May Be Instantiated in a Variety of Ways

It doesn't take much to instantiate a schema. You see a sign that says *Chains Required*, and that's enough to make a schema for *icy roads* pop into your head. You hear, *"All rise,"* spoken out with a flat nasal tone, and—*boom*—your head fills up with a picture of a large room with a gallery for observers, a witness box, a jury box, a judge in black robe, and somebody scrambling to prove her client didn't do it. Very much of the gap-filling activity of natural language is carried along on the back of technical jargon and stock phrases, and verbal competence can be largely measured by how ably one moves about in the world of features they evoke.

Schemas Interact with One Another

If I hear, "Once upon a time, there was a *princess* ...," I get a certain schema in my head. If I hear, "Once upon a time, there was a frog *princess* ...," I get a whole other picture.

Schemas Are Sometimes Self-Referential

The schemas are self-referential to the degree that the sounds of the words themselves are part of what counts for meaning. The most obvious way schemas do this is in *onomatopoeia*. We *zoom* in our cars, we *hush* our children to sleep, we listen to our *boom* boxes. (Well, boom boxes have given way to iPods, but work with me here.) This self-referential aspect of schemas is easily lost in translation.

Another way schemas can be self-referential is in *palindromes*. A palindrome is a word or phrase that reads the same way in both directions, like *Anna* or *Rise to vote, sir*. Here's the coolest palindrome anybody ever wrote. It's Latin, and it means something like, "Arepo the sower holds the wheels at work":

SATOR AREPO TENET OPERA ROTAS.

What makes this the coolest palindrome is that the first letters of the words, taken together, form the first word. The second letters taken together form the second word. The third, the third; the fourth the fourth; and the fifth the fifth. And it does this in both directions! If the main thing about language is to get information out of one head and into another, the loss of the palindrome is insignificant. If the effect on the reader is essential, and not incidental to meaning, the loss of the palindrome represents a significant loss indeed!

Sometimes the same loss is found as we move from Jesus' Aramaic to the Gospels' Greek to our English. For example, in Matthew 23:23-24 Jesus says, "Woe to you, scribes and Pharisees! ... straining out a gnat and swallowing a camel." In Aramaic, the word for *gnat* is *galma*, and the word for *camel* is *gamla*. Jesus made a wordplay: "Woe to you, Scribes and Pharisees! You choke on a louse, but you swallow a house." (All right, I apologize for this. No more rhymes now, I mean it.[3])

Schemas Include Both Connotations and Denotations

Denotations are what you'll find in a dictionary. *Connotations* are the nuanced implications that ride on the backs of the denotations like monkeys. There's a shop near my house where you can buy either of the following signs. Notice the shift of connotation as you move from one to the other:

The first sign says,

> Growing old is natural.
> Growing up is spiritual.

The second sign says,

> Growing old is mandatory.
> Growing up is optional.

In the first sign, *growing up* is the cool thing; it's what you're supposed to aim for. Maturity, stability, all that. In the second, growing up is a trap. Watch out. Stay young as long as possible. Why tell you this? If English is your first language, you could have guessed it for yourself. That's because native speakers of any language recognize the connotations that are packaged up in the schemas of that language. But if English is your second language, you may need some help.

89

Some Schemas Are Morally Loaded

By this we mean that they carry connotations of right and wrong, and good and bad. This is true not only of actions but also of persons, professions, and behaviors. It matters very much whether the film we are watching is *rated* X. When the first century Jew uses the term *Samaritan*, he's likely to spit out the term, much the way a guy in a Conestoga wagon might have spit out the word *Injuns*. (As in, "Circle the wagons, there's *Injuns* comin'.") That's why we switched to *Native American*. (I can use the term *Injuns* this way because I'm part Cherokee. But don't you try it, Paleface. The rules about who can and can't say what are very very complex.)

Schemas Are Multisensory Memories, Not Diagrams

When I diagram a schema on the board, my students are likely to think I mean that when we read a word we instantiate a diagram, but that's not precisely right. The diagrams are ways of charting something that's much more multisensory: Schemas aren't conceptual models so much as organized collections of memories.

When my mechanic hears the word *carburetor*, the schema that comes to his mind is quite complex, and is made up of all sorts of visual, auditory, and physical memories. He knows where carburetors are made, how they should sound, and what they smell like when somebody adjusts the oogleflat the wrong way and screws up the thingamajig.

This is important. Usually, when we think or talk about the language of the Bible—here I'm talking about the schemas in the Bible—we have a natural tendency to stop when we get to the dictionary definition. When somebody in the ancient world read a text, the schemas may very well have throbbed with touch, taste, or emotion.

Consider the word *Passover*. Most of us could offer a pretty good dictionary definition:

> Annual Jewish festival of unleavened bread commemorating the exodus of the Hebrews from Egypt.

I wonder what emotional content the word would have had for a first century Jewish pilgrim, maybe going up to Jerusalem for the first time. The city would have been ablaze with light. The pilgrims in procession would have sung the joyful, resounding choruses of the psalms of ascent.

The city would have been flooded with people, swirling through the streets like rivers, eddying into the alleys and back streets.

Josephus tells us that in AD 65, 255,600 lambs were slaughtered for the Passover celebration in Jerusalem (*War* 6.9.3). Josephus tends to be long on the numbers, and at least one modern interpreter thinks there may have been fewer than 10 percent of that number. Even if we go with the smaller number, imagine for a moment 25,000 lambs being roasted, all on the same day in the confines of a city that was very small by modern standards. I wonder what the air would have smelled like, and how—maybe years later in another part of the Mediterranean basin—a Jewish traveler might smell a lamb on the spit and be carried back to Passover in Jerusalem.

Suppose now that that Jew is experiencing the smell of that lamb in the fall of AD 70, right after Jerusalem has been sacked and burned by the Romans, and its temple left in smoldering ruins. What sorrows would that smell have carried with it?

The point of this exercise is that if I look up the Greek word *pascha* and learn that it means *Passover*, and then I look up the word *Passover* in an English dictionary, I still may not have finished my work. In addition to careful, exacting research, we need to bring informed and sympathetic imagination to bear. The mind—and therefore understanding—does not exist as pure, abstract, logical thought. The mind involves emotions, muscle memories, gut reactions, fears. Some words don't only *signify;* they *throb.* In ordinary language—the language we talk every day—significant dimensions of meaning are packaged up in the sheer palpitation of the words and the emotional content they evoke.

Schemas Are Built by Experience, As Needed

In our heads, schemas are not ready-packaged and complete, but are constantly growing and changing as we learn new things. They start out small and then are built up, developed, and corrected as we learn more stuff. I was in my twenties before my schema for *duck* included a node that says, *has wicked bite.* The connections are reinforced by repetition or by the vividness and clarity of the experiences that produced them. Now my schema for *eating duck* contains a very vivid node for *revenge.* The more frequent or more forceful the reinforcement, the more prominent those features will be in the memory.

Schemas Differ from One Language to Another

Bottom line: If the schemas are built up by experience as needed, and if they're made of memories and not diagrams or abstract concepts, they automatically differ from one language to another. Since speakers of different languages often have different real experiences of the world, their schemas will differ too. My schema for *pig* includes a node for *taste*, which a first-century Jew would have found impossible to imagine. For a first-century Jew, the schema for *pig* is tagged for taboo: Pigs are part of a category called *animals that must not be eaten*. When we simply translate word for word, we can easily overlook subsidiary nodes of information that are found in the schemas of the original language but not in the schemas of the receptor language. This also means that the schemas of Greek words will be organized differently from the schemas of corresponding English words. What is common and therefore central in Greek experience may be rare and therefore peripheral in English. Sometimes those subsidiary nodes of information are precisely the point.

Advances in technology can also change schemas. Some ancient Greek guy hears the word *kosmos*, and he tries to get a picture of the cosmos in his head. Notice that there's no good old U.S. of A. in his world map. There is no Hubble telescope picture of Mother Earth, suspended in space. But we do have such pictures, and they're awe inspiring. It's hard for us to ignore them; but if we want to read the Bible the way an original reader would have, we have to picture the smaller image of the *kosmos* our ancient Greek guy had in his head.

To get at the way he understood time, we have to imagine a world without mechanical clocks. Our word *hour* designates a period of time comprised of sixty identical minutes. In each day there are precisely twenty-four of these. In the ancient world, an *hour* consisted of one-twelfth of the period between sunrise and sunset. As the seasons changed, the length of an hour varied accordingly, with the hours being shorter in winter and longer in summer; and the only place where hours were identical was on the equator. Everywhere else, the length of the hour varied with the length of the day, and on no two consecutive days were the hours the same length. Talk about *flex*-time.

An Experiment in Schema Building

It may be helpful at this point to apply this discussion to the biblical literature itself, since that's really what we're talking about. One of the clearest ways in which schemas function is when they introduce analogies—"this is like that." Notice, however, that for an analogy to function correctly, the listener is supposed to bring a couple of schemas to the listening. Suppose the analogy says,

> That went over like a lead balloon.

To get this, we have to access schemas for *that* (the implied antecedent of the pronoun), for *lead,* and for *balloon.* The expression *lead balloon* is oxymoronic, it's self-contradictory; and the reader knows it isn't supposed to be taken literally. This gives a secondary meaning to the opening verbal complex, "went over." What's in view is a crash.

By the same token, in Mark 10:15, Jesus says,

> Whoever does not receive the kingdom of God like a little child, shall not enter it.

In order to get this, Mark's readers are expected to summon up a schema for *receiving the kingdom of God* and one for *child,* and then decide which features are shared between them. In a short study of this verse, Richard White explores the ways in which the modern interpreter can short-circuit the exegetical task by assuming that the schema for *child* has the same features in Greek that it has in English.[4] These include trust, dependence, obedience, innocence, and so forth. Thus, "the preacher's fertile imagination and acculturation dictate a whole catalogue of virtues personified by the ideal child."[5]

Yet—and here's the rub—"what everybody believed in first-century Palestine is not what everybody believes now—at least not on this subject.... Jesus was assuming that everyone knew children were 'trivial,' 'weak' and 'poor,' 'having no standing' and 'come empty-handed like a beggar.'"[6] This emphasis on coming to the kingdom empty-handed is, of course, something we see quite readily in other passages of scripture in which Jesus insists that the kingdom comes to the outcast. Why, asks White, do we miss it so often in this passage? The answer is that although the Greek word *paidion* really does mean "child" (and although this is an exactly proper translation), the Greek word instantiates a very different schema, with a very different range of features.

93

Unless we get the schemas right, we may miss what the Bible is actually saying, and—worse—we may attribute meanings to the biblical text that aren't actually there. When we do that, we may end up giving our own ideas biblical authority. On the other hand, as we learn about ancient schemas, the Bible slips from black and white to color. So does our Christian faith.

Side Note: A Word about Expertise

This is a good place to think about what it means to become an expert at something. It's a coincidence that a schema looks a little like the roots of a tree. Every time you learn something new about a schema, you add a tiny root line that wasn't there before so that you gradually build up a thickly tangled root ball.

My mechanic is an expert car guy. His schema for the word *carburetor* is thickly developed, like this:

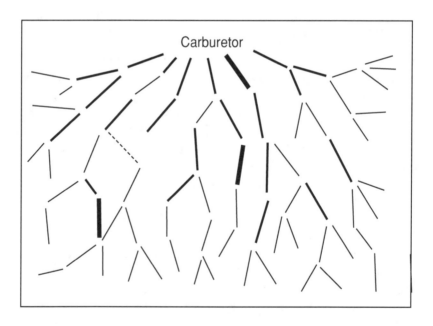

Figure 7.3

I'm a klutz with engines. My schema for *carburetor* is so small it hardly takes up any space at all. My schema looks like this:

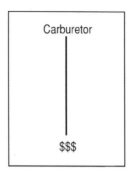

I have a very tiny schema for the word *airwalking*. I think it's some kind of skateboard stunt where you move your feet back and forth while they're off the board. Dylan, the kid across the street, has a thickly developed schema for *airwalking*. He also knows about the *Airwalk* brand of skateboard shoes, while I've never heard of those. His schema is the Hummer of schemas; mine doesn't even have wheels.

When my mechanic calls his parts supplier, the exchange of information between them is both richer and clearer than it is when either one of them talks to me. I require a lot of explanatory asides. Because the only node in my schema for carburetor looks like dollar signs, I also need more reassurances. But suppose my mechanic and his parts guy only had my vocabulary with which to talk shop. They'd never get anything done. This suggests something important: the technical vocabulary experts use is an important part of their work; it helps them talk shop with speed, efficiency, and precision. The downside of that truth is that their shoptalk leaves me out.

This is also true when we move to experts in the biblical literature. Say I'm a beginning text critic, learning about NT manuscripts. I learn that some variant is supported by *Codex Sinaiticus*. The word *codex* tips me off that it's bound as a book, rather than as a scroll, and I might read somewhere that it's a fourth century manuscript. That's enough for me to use the word in a conversation and not feel like a total doofus. But suppose I mention Codex Sinaiticus in a conversation with somebody like my friend Gordon Fee.[7] Dr. Fee knows this codex like the back of his hand because he's studied it under a microscope. His schema is richly developed, and includes hundreds (maybe thousands) of details of information, like my mechanic's schema for *carburetor*.

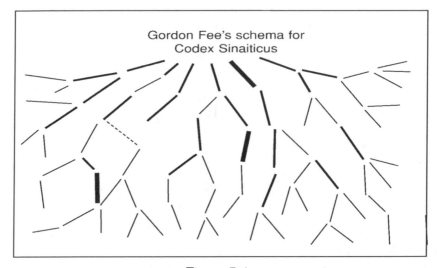

Figure 7.4

Not only that, but Dr. Fee's schema has a network of entanglements with other schemas that I don't know anything about—like the roots of a stand of redwood trees, entangled together as the trees grow.

When Dr. Fee gets together with other text critics to talk shop, they need this precise vocabulary in order to do business with precision and economy of movement. I've been in the room when this happens, and I can tell you as an ear-witness, the place can crackle with data as it gets tapped and zapped between the experts.

This explains why scholars are sometimes puzzled when people insist that scholarship is a hindrance to understanding the Bible, or when people insist that the academic jargon of the discipline is unnecessary. We hear that a lot, and it's a little discouraging. What people forget is that the translation they hold in their hands is the work of experts who sometimes invested years of their lives learning the schemas necessary to do their work. If the experts didn't have a technical vocabulary, they wouldn't be able to do their work at all. The jargon has its place because it enables experts to share information efficiently, with precision and economy of movement, like my mechanic and his parts supplier.

Now, in a sense, as we grow up in a culture, over time we become "expert" in the schemas that are part of the common knowledge of the culture. That's one of the reasons why we go to school—to learn schemas. But these will differ from time to time, and from place to place. A Native

American kid on the open prairie, growing up in the 1860s, will need to learn a lot more about buffalo than a kid growing up in New York City at the same time. Kicking Bear doesn't even know there *is* a New York City. He doesn't know, and he doesn't care. He wouldn't have had any way to know that it's the 1860s, either, but that's okay too because he doesn't care about that either. Remember the movie *Dances With Wolves*? As we move from the twenty-first century back to the first, we're like John J. Dunbar learning how to think like Dances With Wolves. We have to go back and learn what those schemas would have been like for somebody who grew up in that culture.

To Sum Up

What we learned in this chapter is that the mind organizes experience into schemas and then taps those as it needs to in order to fill in gaps in the language of the text. We also learned that schemas differ from language to language. So how do we learn about the schemas of the Bible? We use a specialized paradigm called *Lexicography*, to which we turn in chapter 8.

Chapter 8

How We Find Out about Schemas

The Discipline of Lexicography

Lexicographer: A writer of dictionaries, a harmless drudge.
—Samuel Johnson,
Johnson's Dictionary

We find out about basic schemas from the discipline of *Lexicography*, more commonly known as "word study." It's the easiest kind of Bible study to do. It's also the easiest to mess up. The point of word study is to reconstruct the schemas the ancient authors expected their readers to instantiate. Only after that can we ask what English term or concept to use in translation. The problem is, we have to learn this at a distance of 2,000 years, and there isn't anybody who speaks Koine Greek as a first language whom we can ask for clues. This means we have to develop a credible historical method to get it right.

First, a Little Theory

In one sense, lexicographers learn about schemas in exactly the same way we all learned to talk: We pay attention to the way the words are used in context. If a word is common in the language, it doesn't take very long before we see patterns, and these patterns show what the word means.

Suppose we're reading "The Man with the Twisted Lip," which is one of Arthur Conan Doyle's wonderful stories about Sherlock Holmes. We pick up the story at a point where Holmes dashes out of his famous flat at 221B Baker Street:

- "And so in ten minutes I had left my armchair and cheery sitting-room behind me, and was speeding eastward in a *hansom* on a strange errand, as it seemed to me at the time, though the future only could show how strange it was to be."

We haven't seen this word *hansom* before, but from the context it appears that it must be a kind of taxi-cab. But we want to check, to be sure, so we get a Holmes concordance, which would list all the words and tell where they're found. A quick check of those other places confirms that we're close:

- "I have the advantage of knowing your habits, my dear Watson," said he. "When your round is a short one you walk, and when it is a long one you use a *hansom*. As I perceive that your boots, although used, are by no means dirty, I cannot doubt that you are at present busy enough to justify the *hansom*." (From "The Crooked Man")
- "In the morning you will send for a *hansom*, desiring your man to take neither the first nor the second which may present itself. Into this *hansom* you will jump, and you will drive to the Strand end of the Lowther Arcade, handing the address to the cabman upon a slip of paper, with a request that he will not throw it away. Have your fare ready, and the instant that your cab stops, dash through the Arcade, timing yourself to reach the other side at a quarter-past nine." (From "The Final Problem")

So a *hansom* is a taxicab. Since we know that the Sherlock Holmes stories were set in the nineteenth century, it's a sure bet the cab is horse-drawn, rather than motorized. There's more to learn (a *hansom* had two wheels, rather than four, which we would not have guessed from these examples), but we've learned enough to make a sensible reading of Holmes. The more such references we find, the more things we learn about the schema, and the more we can be certain that we've gotten to the right meaning.

Hapax Legomena

But what do we do about words that only appear a single time? A word that appears only once is called a *hapax legomenon* (plural: *hapax legomena*), from the Greek words *hapax*, which means *once*, and *legomenon*, which means *spoken*. It's not uncommon to read in a commentary that some word is "*hapax* in Paul," which means that in all of Paul's writings this word only appears one time. Something can be hapax in Paul, but common everywhere else. Or hapax in the NT, or hapax in all of ancient literature. How do we discover the meaning of hapaxes?

Parallels—Positive and Negative

One way is to see if the word appears in a parallel of some kind. For example, in Matthew 5:17, Jesus says,

"Do not think that I have come to abolish the law and the prophets.
    I came not   to   abolish,
    But   (to) *plerosai* . . . "

What does *plerosai* mean here? From the negative parallel, it's a fair guess that here it has to mean the opposite of *abolish*, so we might translate, *establish*.

Etymology

A second way to check out a *hapax legomenon* is to see if it's derived from words we do know. Suppose you're reading some novel when you came across the following sentence:

• The city spread out before him in all of its chryselephantine splendor.

You've never seen the word *chryselephantine* before, but if you knew that the Greek word *chrysas* meant *gold* and the word *elephantinos* meant *ivory*, you could put the two meanings together and come up with a meaning that pretty much fits the context. You look the word up later just to be sure, and learn that *chryselephantine* means "studded with gold and ivory."

Actually, we use etymology a lot to get at the meaning of new words. Jack Handey's *deep thought* about the word *mankind* depends for its depth on our knowing how whacked out it is:

- Maybe in order to understand mankind, we have to look at the word itself: "*Mankind*." Basically, it's made up of two separate words—"*mank*" and "*ind*". What do these words mean? It's a mystery, and that's why so is mankind.

Translations out of the OT

When we're dealing with hapaxes in the Bible, ancient translations can be enormously helpful. A word may be hapax in the NT, but found in the Septuagint (the Greek OT used by the writers of the NT; abbreviation: LXX). When that happens, we can discover what Hebrew word it translates, and in that way learn a little more of its meaning.

Translations into Syriac and Latin

The same consideration can be turned on its head. A lexicographer can study the ways the Greek word was translated into Syriac or Latin. The assumption here is that just because a word is *hapax* in the Bible, that doesn't mean nobody ever spoke that word in conversation. It might very well have been part of the common talk, and therefore perfectly clear to an early translator.

Combining These Strategies

Lexicographers don't use these strategies only with hapaxes; they use them with common words too. (In fact, my example *plerosai*, above, is quite common.) So Step One for the lexicographer is just to collect the evidence, including various places in which the word is used, the evidence from parallelism, the ways it was translated by Latin or Syriac, the Hebrew word or words it translated in the Septuagint, and its derivation (or etymology).

Step Two is to sort the evidence, looking for patterns. Picture a lexicographer named Carole sitting at a desk with a stack of index cards, all of them dealing with the Greek word *plerosai* (fulfill). Each card contains a record of one place where *plerosai* occurs in the ancient literature. Some of the cards are scribbled over with notes:

- Appears in conjunction with prophecy: "Such and such happened to fulfill (*plerosai*) what had been spoken by the prophet."
- Contrasting parallel with *katalusai* (destroy).
- Used to describe a net full of fish.
- Jesus uses this word when he tells John the Baptist that this must happen "to fulfill (*plerosai*) all righteousness."

Things like that. She shuffles the cards and then begins laying them out on the desk in what looks like a game of solitaire. This goes here. No, there. This one here. It's slow, exacting work, but in this way she begins to quantify the evidence as a way of certifying that the patterns are really there. Then she sifts through each stack, double-checking the patterns. As she works, here are the kinds of questions she asks:

- How is the word used generally?
- What components go into the makeup of the word? Where did it come from? What are its parts?
- How do context and grammar affect the way the word is used?
- What's the significance of the sound of the word? Is it used in wordplays and puns, for example?
- Is the word part of a technical vocabulary, and if so, what does it mean in that context? Is it loaded in some way?
- In each instance that it occurs, what does it connote?
- If the word appears in the Greek translation of the OT, what Hebrew word did it translate? How was it translated into Latin or Syriac?

These are the sorts of things Carole reports as the results of her word study.

Diachronic Lexicography

Suppose Carole put a date next to each occurrence of the word, and then laid the cards out chronologically. What she would discover is that the word has shifted meaning over time. We call this aspect of word study *diachronic* study, from the Greek words *dia* (which means *through*) and *chronos* (which means *time*). We shouldn't be surprised by diachronic changes in word meanings. Lots of factors force words to change meanings.

Carole may discover, for example, that during the period of the NT the word *martyrein* originally meant *to bear witness*, and it didn't acquire the meaning *to die for one's faith* until later, after the period of the NT has closed. When Carole adds that to her notes, what she's doing is establishing a check against reading later meanings back into earlier occurrences of the word.

I suppose that if we were to trace the historical origins of every word spoken by a community and learn what factors caused some words to drop out or change meanings, we would have a pretty good social history of that community. During my lifetime, a whole bunch of new words have landed on our linguistic plates. PDA (which used to mean *public display of affection*, but now also means *personal digital assistant*). RAM. Intel. Quark. Supernova. When Katie Couric says in an interview, "So what's the 4-1-1 on that, anyway?" we all know she's asking for information, but the same question wouldn't have made any sense in 1949.

Synchronic Lexicography

If Carole evaluates all of the possible meanings of a word *at a given moment in time*, we say she's studying the word *synchronically*. Imagine that the word is a long tube, stretching out backwards and forwards over a period of decades, or even centuries. Inside the tube, the word expands and contracts, gains popularity, falls into disuse, and shifts meaning.

Now, if Carole examines the whole tube, she's doing a *diachronic* study, but if she slices it across the middle with a knife like a loaf of bread and looks at one moment in time, her study is *synchronic*.

So What's Next?

Suppose we take our new skill with word study and apply it to one of Jack Handey's *deep thoughts*:

- I think a good gift for the president would be a chocolate revolver. And since he's so busy, you'd probably have to run up to him real quick and hand it to him.

It's easy enough to discover that the word *revolver* means a handgun of some sort. A comprehensive study of the use of the word in English would leave us certain of its meaning, but puzzled by the adjective *chocolate*. And what does that have to do with the president? It's all very puzzling.

Clearly the word study isn't enough. If we're going to *get* this saying, we have to bring in information about who the president is, and about the Secret Service people, and about people having to pass through metal detectors and all sorts of stuff about security. That is, to understand this saying, we have to know how people do business. We turn to that stuff in chapter 9.

So How Do I Find Out More about This Topic?

Aside from the original texts themselves, lexicographers work with two primary tools—lexicons and concordances. These vary widely, so I'll just make some preliminary suggestions. Frederick Danker provides further direction; see: *Multipurpose Tools for Bible Study* (Minneapolis: Fortress, 1993). D. A. Carson offers useful cautions about how to use these tools: *Exegetical Fallacies* (Grand Rapids: Baker, 1984). The Lexus of lexicons is edited by Gerhard Kittel and Gerhard Friedrich, *Theological Dictionary of the New Testament* (trans. Geoffrey W. Bromiley; 10 vols.; Grand Rapids: Eerdmans, 1964–1976). This set—which scholars simply call "Kittel" or TDNT—is truly massive, a wonderful resource. But sometimes less is more, so the translator Geoffrey Bromiley cut it down into a handy single volume: *Theological Dictionary of the New Testament Abridged in One Volume* (Grand Rapids: Eerdmans, 1985).

Chapter 9

HOW WE FIND OUT ABOUT CULTURAL KNOWLEDGE AND PRACTICES

The Discipline of Backgrounds

So the first way we fill in gaps is with basic schemas, which we learn from the discipline of Lexicography. The second way is with *cultural knowledge*, which we learn from the discipline of *Backgrounds*. Suppose my friend David slaps me on the back in the hallway and says,

> "Did you hear the one about the two old ladies who took a fifth of whiskey to the baseball game?"

Everything I know about the body language (slap on the back), the context (hallway, rather than board room), and David (funny guy) suggests that there's a joke coming. That expectation is validated by the genre signal ("Did you hear the one about ... ?"). In the joke there will be dissonances, and I will know to let them stand rather than resolve them in one direction or another. He has posed the question. I know from the genre signals that the appropriate answer is to claim ignorance.

> "No," I tell him. "What about the two old ladies who took the fifth of whiskey to the baseball game?"

He follows up with the punch line:

"At the bottom of the fifth the bags were loaded."

Let's list the specific information I have to have known in advance if I'm going to laugh at David's joke.

- That *old ladies* are sometimes called *bags*. So are *bases*.
- That baseball is divided into innings, and that *the bottom of the fifth* a technical term for a moment at play.
- That whiskey comes in units of a fifth of a gallon.
- That whiskey is alcoholic, and that *loaded* is slang for *drunk*.
- That the expression, *the bags were loaded*, refers to a situation in play in which there's a player on every base.

Not only do I have to know this stuff, I have to know it in advance, and I have to use it in particular ways. If I tell David's joke to my students, there are two groups who don't usually laugh—students who have heard it before and English-as-Second-Language students. If we've heard it before, the punch line doesn't punch; and if we're ESL students, we may have flawless diction and perfect pronunciation, but still not know enough about American slang or baseball to realize that there's a punch line to laugh at.

In a sense, when we turn to the biblical stories, we're crippled in both ways. We've heard it all before, so the surprises are crippled. And what we've heard tends not to take an adequate accounting of the cultural background. We're Greek-as-Second-Language students.

Cultural Literacy

David's joke brings us to something sociologists have lately begun to call *cultural literacy*. This has to do with information that writers expect their readers to know already, simply because they grew up in the same culture. Here are some examples: customs; rules and expectations of etiquette; jurisprudence; science; distances and geography; procedures of production and manufacture; laws; information about how to deal with witches; folk remedies; information about agriculture, seasons, and the condition of the roads during the rainy season; details about historical events, migrations, personal and social dynamics; beliefs about society and about human nature; beliefs about the supernatural. What's normal for breakfast? Does a student stand or sit in the presence of a respected teacher? How long does a wedding take?

We could go on and on with this list because it's nearly endless. Readers are expected to draw freely from this body of cultural knowledge as part of their basic gap filling. This information too is organized as hierarchies of information—in schematic form—though those schemas may be larger and more complex than the basic schemas of individual words.

Here's a good place to practice being aware that we also naturally tend to default to what we've always been told. Once I visited Israel in January and was surprised by a deep cold snap. I asked the guide, "How did they keep their feet warm, wearing sandals and all?" I'll never forget her response: "You Americans are so provincial," she said. "You imagine us in perpetual summer because that's when your film crews come here. Did it never occur to you that they might have known how to make boots?"

So now I've got this picture in my head—Jesus in boots! But why not? Would he be less the Son of God if he wore boots? The bottom line here is that when we're questing for Jesus we should avoid superimposing modern ideas and images back on history unless we have clear warrants for doing so.

Scripts

If the schemas have role expectations embedded within them, they're called *scripts*. Scripts tell us how to act in specific social situations. (There's a specific script for what you do when a police car pulls up behind you and the officer turns on the red flashing light.)

Suppose the story begins by identifying the scene as *dinner out at a restaurant*, the writer will expect the reader to know that this involves sitting together at a table, being approached by a waiter or waitress, ordering from a menu, leaving a tip, and paying for the meal with an overburdened credit card. Usually these come in a predictable sequence. They are scripted activities, in which the characters are playing roles that were written and directed by society at large.

By contrast, in first century Palestine the script *dinner party* was organized on a very different order. The primary movements of the story about the anointing of Jesus (Luke 7:36-50) rest upon the reader's knowledge of that script: When the guests arrive, they leave their sandals at the door; there is an exchange of kisses; the host is supposed to see that the guests' feet are washed; guests recline at the table, with their feet extended out behind them; village folk are permitted to observe from the perimeters of the room; and so forth.

These are common courtesies. The kiss—or perhaps an embrace—is a way of recognizing the status of the guest. The foot washing is an important gesture in a culture where everyone wore sandals and trudged along dirt roads. A thoughtful host was expected to offer his guests a little oil for their skin, to counter the effects of the blistering sun. It was only common courtesy.

This is the script Luke expected his reader to bring to the story. Notice the way the host in the story has violated the script:

> I entered your house, *you gave me no water for my feet,* but she has wet my feet with her tears and wiped them with her hair. *You gave me no kiss,* but from the time I came in she has not ceased to kiss my feet. *You did not anoint my head with oil,* but she has anointed my feet with ointment. (vv. 44-46, emphasis added)

This is a little like inviting you to be a guest in my home and then neglecting to take your hat and coat at the door. Or mixing up our good china with the ordinary dishes and sitting you at a place with the ordinary dishes. So against the backdrop of the normal script, it appears the host has insulted Jesus.

The insult in turn may explain why the woman was crying. Perhaps she was moved by compassion for Jesus. Maybe. We can't know for sure. If she was, though, it would explain why she did what she did. She did it to correct the insult. It was awkward and embarrassing, and it was misunderstood, but it was a gesture that came from good intentions.

Imagine too the way this would embarrass the host. He's the rich guy, he's the host, and it takes a woman of the streets to do right by Jesus. The host turns his embarrassment the wrong way: All he can think about is the fact that Jesus lets himself be touched by a woman with a bad reputation.

What Role Does Cultural Knowledge Play in Exegesis?

So far as exegesis is concerned, cultural information plays two important roles.

It Helps the Reader Fill in Gaps

First, *scripts add information to the reader's literary repertoire*. In the right context, a single word or phrase can summon up an entire set of stock expectations and responses, against which the details of the plot unfold, just as "All rise" can conjure up an image of a courtroom.

Violations of Norms Call Attention to Themselves

Second, cultural information provides a way for writers to create emphasis. That's because *violations of the norms call attention to themselves*. Notice that this can work only if the right cultural information is instantiated. That's why skill with cultural norms is a critical aspect of competent reading, and therefore of competent exegesis. There is no literacy without cultural literacy.

It's the violations of the scripts that create the punch in Luke's story of the anointing of Jesus. This is a good place to stop and read that story. As you read, notice that Luke waited until the end of the story before he told his readers that the host had insulted Jesus. In the meantime, the readers default to the norm and read as though the host has fulfilled all of his responsibilities to his guest. The delayed timing gives the story a significant reversal, which functions as a kind of trap for the reader. Believing that the host has done right by Jesus, the readers won't have any context in which to understand why the woman does what she does. This nudges them toward being shocked at her behavior, and at Jesus for not stopping her. To the extent that the readers share the host's shock, Jesus' words to the host may also be directed to the readers too:

> "A certain creditor had two debtors; one owed five hundred denarii, and the other fifty. When they could not pay, he forgave them both. Now which of them will love him more? Simon answered, "The one, I suppose, to whom he forgave more." And he said to him, "You have judged rightly." Then turning toward the woman, he said to Simon, "Do you see this woman? I entered your house, you gave me no water for my feet, but she has wet my feet with her tears and wiped them with her hair. You gave me no kiss, but from the time I came in she has not ceased to kiss my feet. You did not anoint my head with oil, but she has anointed my feet with ointment. Therefore, I tell you, her sins, which are many, have been forgiven, for she loved much; but he who is forgiven little, loves little." (7:41–47)

111

The story is a scorpion: The sting comes in the tail.

Although we're often unaware of it, most of our social interaction is scripted out in these ways. Like other schemas, the scripts are constructed with typicality as their primary organizing feature. The typicality means that the ritual dances of life are choreographed by social experience. We earn our place in the dance troupe by copying the principal dancers who went before us—where they wheel and turn, how they execute their pirouette, and when they stop and bow. In return for our trouble, we can proceed with the confidence that when we perform the *pas de deux*, we will be in step and our partner will not trip us.

So What Else Do I Need to Know?

Sooner or later as we study cultural practices, we discover that they're backed up by assumptions about right and wrong. Cultural information is seldom neutral information. There's a right way to do things, and there's a wrong way, and writers expect us to share their judgments about right and wrong. This raises the question of cultural norms, to which we turn in chapter 10.

So How Do I Find Out More about This Topic?

Generally speaking, the fastest way to find out about cultural backgrounds is to check out the commentaries. It's probably best to steer clear of devotional commentaries for this purpose, because these have a different intent and so deal with background more loosely. There are also very good volumes that deal specifically with cultural and historical backgrounds. One of the easiest to use is by Craig Keener, *The IVP Bible Background Commentary: New Testament* (Downers Grove: InterVarsity, 1993).

Here are some other titles you may find helpful: Everett Fergusen, *Backgrounds of Early Christianity* (Grand Rapids: Eerdmans, 1993); William Horbury, *Messianism Among Jews and Christians: Biblical and Historical Studies* (London: T & T Clark, 2003); Hans-Josef Klauck, *The Religious Context of Early Christianity: A Guide to Graeco-Roman Religion*

(Minneapolis: Fortress, 2003); Victor Matthews, *Manners and Customs in the Bible: An Illustrated Guide to Daily Life in Bible Times* (Peabody, Mass.: Hendrickson, 1988); George W. E. Nickelsburg, *Ancient Judaism and Christian Origins: Diversity, Continuity, and Transformation* (Minneapolis: Fortress, 2003), and *Jewish Literature Between the Bible and the Mishnah: A Literary and Historical Introduction* (2nd ed. Minneapolis: Fortress, 2005); Ralph Martin Novak, *Christianity and the Roman Empire: Background Texts* (Harrisburg, Pa.: Trinity Press, 2001); Oskar Skarsaune, *In the Shadow of the Temple: Jewish Influences on Early Christianity* (Downers Grove: InterVarsity, 2003); and Peter Tomson, *"If This Be from Heaven . . ." Jesus and the New Testament Authors in their Relationship to Judaism* (Sheffield: Sheffield Academic Press, 2001).

Chapter 10

How We Find Out about Cultural Norms

The Discipline of Social Science

Chapter 9 dealt with the fact that texts presuppose a lot of cultural information that readers are expected to have in hand when they begin reading. But, we said, cultural information is seldom neutral information and writers expect their readers to share their judgments about right and wrong, so we have to begin this chapter by refining what we learned in the last one: writers expect their readers to share the *rhetorical assumptions* on which their ideas about right and wrong can be argued.

In the story *The Sea and Little Fishes*, Terry Pratchett creates an entirely believable and comical world of kindly witches who grow old, exchange gifts, form personal alliances, and compete for prizes in the annual magic competition. The alliances are developed in tiny conversations, in which they snipe at each other behind each other's back. In the following clip, pay attention not to what the speaker says but to what she assumes as the basis of what she says:

> "The woman married a wizard," says Esmée Weatherwax. "*You can't tell me that's right.*"

Notice what this gossip assumes on the part of its listener—that witches who marry wizards are breaking some agreed-upon code that "everybody knows is right." For this reason, rhetorical assumptions are crucial to the inner logic of a text, and are important clues to its author's intention.

Introducing Cultural Norms

This leads to an important consideration in the interpretation of the Bible: Not all cultures sort out right and wrong in the same ways. In Southern California where I live, we just don't care if witches marry wizards. The point here is that that native sense of right and wrong isn't entirely "objective," but is taught and learned within a culture, and different cultures set the boundaries in very different places.

In the book *Into the Heart*, anthropologist Kenneth Good tells the story of the Yanomama Indians in the Amazon basin of Brazil. Good spent eight years living and working among the Yanomama. Early in his stay in one of the villages, the chief offered him his daughter Yarima in marriage, an offer which Good accepted. In time, and after a fair amount of personal wrestling, Good decided to take his new bride out of the Amazon basin.

> Yarima's father objected. "*Nubahs*," he said, using the Yanomama word for outsider. "Not civilized."
>
> "Why not?"
>
> "*Nubahs* don't even drink the ashes of their dead ancestors. How can they be civilized?"[1]

What makes this example interesting is that Yarima's father simply assumed that Good would agree. Everybody knows that it's barbaric to dishonor your dead by burying them in the ground. The *proper* thing to do is to cremate the body and mix the ashes into a banana drink. Only yahoos and moral idiots—*nubahs*—would fail to do that.

Norms Are Taken for Granted

I tried this same argument to prevent my kids from going to Massachusetts to attend college and graduate school. It didn't work. Not only did it not work but my kids didn't have to tell me why. Norms generally don't need to be voiced. It's not just that we have norms, but that we generally don't come to norms by having a rational discussion and then voting. Rather, we learn norms by listening to our parents talk when we're little, or by watching what happens to people who get out of line.[2] Yarima's father believed—that is, he took for granted—that drinking the ashes of one's ancestors is simply good etiquette, and that anybody who failed to do that was disrespectful and rude. Skipping that is just not the done thing. His argument was based on what he supposed would be a shared understanding about right and wrong.

Cultural Norms and the Bible

Let's consider what norms mean for our reading of the Bible. If different cultures have different shared understandings about right and wrong, we can't simply take it for granted that the norms for American culture will be the same as the norms that were taken for granted by the people who wrote the Bible.

The OT tells this terrible story about King David (2 Sam 11). We all know the drill here. David sends his guys off to battle, but he himself stays home, where he gets in trouble with his neighbor's wife. (Smart king, but apparently not good on long-range planning.) The chapter ends with this simple, stunning comment by the narrator: "The thing that David had done displeased the LORD" (v. 27).

But the narrator didn't really need to tell us that what David did had displeased the LORD. Even in English, we can see that the LORD's displeasure drips from the story like arsenic. That's because David violates a lot of cultural norms that we also share: All that stuff about adultery and murder; the treacherous way he trots Uriah back to battle carrying his own death warrant; the complicity of David's henchman, Joab. It's sleazy stuff all the way around. What makes it worse is an assumption we do not share, that most of us would think rather odd: *A soldier must not, under any circumstances, engage in sexual activity during wartime.* Not with his own wife, not with a prostitute, not with somebody else's wife even if you're the king (!), not with nobody.

Enter Social Science

The discipline that deals with cultural norms is called *Social Science.* While the Social Sciences are more than one hundred years old (they actually go back to the Renaissance), it has only been in the past thirty years or so that Social Science perspectives have been used to help understand the Bible. (Actually, this stuff was introduced in the 1930s, faltered, and then has exploded since the mid-1970s).

Technically, Social-Science research is closely related to Bible Backgrounds, but it moves beyond traditional approaches to Backgrounds in two particular ways. First, it pushes beyond cataloging cultural practices. It's important to know how long a marriage feast might last, or what you serve your guests, or what the marriageable age might be, or how a marriage might be arranged; but it's also important to know what such things meant to the overall social structure, and what they meant to the individuals who lived within it. The discipline of Backgrounds asks *what* people did; the Social Sciences ask *why* they did it.

Second, in order to discover this deeper stratum of information, the social scientists have had to develop more nuanced and subtle methods of evaluation. Social scientists generally fall into two somewhat different groups.

Anthropologists study a given culture by immersing themselves in it. (This is the approach taken by Kenneth Good when he went to live with the Yanomama Indians.) Immersion is a good way to arrive at a thick analysis of the details of social life. For that reason, anthropology is better suited for studying small, compact societies, or groups within larger cultural units.

Sociologists tend to do their work with statistics, looking for patterns over large bodies of evidence. For that reason, sociology is better suited for studying whole cultures.

Each of these approaches faces a problem when we come to the cultures of the Bible. We can't go back and live there (which frustrates the anthropologists), and our statistical data is very limited and often biased, incomplete, or simply blown all out of whack by prejudiced recordkeeping (which frustrates the sociologists). So what to do? Is there some way to finesse the evidence we do have to make it tell us stuff about cultural norms it wasn't intending to tell? And if we could do that, would it provide additional clues about the meaning of the things it *does* intend to tell?

Analogies with Contemporary Cultures

One approach is to find comparable cultures that exist today to study how these cultures resolve problems and what they take for granted. So we study Arab villages, or we sit down with Afghan elders and ask them right from wrong. We find cultures where people live in roughly the same living conditions—same diet, same access to health care, same sanitation—and we discover what their mortality rate is. Then we study how their social structures are different because of this mortality rate. This can help us clarify the kinds of questions we might bring to the biblical evidence.

This approach is tricky though, because it runs the risk of reading modern information back into the text. Advocates of this approach have a ready reply to this objection: first, this is a paradigm that forces our own taken-for-granted world into the open, and that's a good thing. Second, by studying what patterns emerge in modern parallel contexts, we can use what we learn to reframe the questions we bring to the biblical text. With better questions, we're more likely to notice corroborating—or disconfirming!—evidence within the ancient literature, and we end up where we want to be.

A second approach is to restrict our observations to the ancient literature itself, looking for patterns. There are several ways of doing this. Let's look more closely.

Prosopography

One way social scientists study patterns in the literature is called *prosopography*. This is "evidence taken at face value," from the Greek word *prosopon*, which means "face." A primary source for prosopographic evidence is names, and sometimes the relationships that can be discerned between names and social roles.

Once, in the Sunday paper I read an editorial piece about a Supreme Court ruling on abortion. The writer's name was Francis X. O'Connor. Even before I read the article, I knew Mr. O'Connor would be pro-life. How did I know that? Because I knew he had been raised in a strict Irish-Catholic home. How did I know that? Well, what would the initial X stand for? Limited range of options, but Xavier presents itself. Put Xavier together with Francis and we get the name, Francis Xavier. It was Francis Xavier who, along with Ignatius of Loyola, founded the Society of Jesus— the Jesuits. Protestant parents rarely name their children after Francis Xavier, but devout Irish Catholic parents often do.

Notice that I was dealing here with probabilities. (Did you notice the series of logical inferences here?) The facts might very well have been different. Perhaps Mr. and Mrs. O'Connor had been scam artists who named their baby Francis Xavier after a wealthy grandfather in the hope that old Granddad would think kindly of him and leave him part of his stash. Perhaps Mr. F. X. O'Connor was raised Catholic, but had quit the faith and was now a pro-choice activist. (Could happen. Less likely.) But all in all, the odds were good that he was still Catholic, and still pro-life. Indeed, if the article turned out to be pro-choice, we could infer with some confidence that Mr. O'Connor was a renegade from the religion of his family.

We deal with this matter of probability this way: We look for patterns, and then from those patterns begin to weave together images of daily life. Suppose we take a name like *Onesimus*, which means *useful*. That throws the likelihood on the side that he was born a slave. Now, we have a way of checking: we can learn what we can about other people in the ancient world named Onesimus; and lo and behold, if they were all slaves, we've got a pattern. We may be onto something. The more widespread the pattern appears, the more likely that the generality will be valid.

Explanatory Power

We can also look for what could be called *explanatory power*. (The technical word for this is *heuristic* power.) We're dealing with ancient evidence, which is missing parts because things decay or get lost. That means that a lot of the historian's work is filling in the gaps in the evidence the way a CSI detective fills in gaps in the evidence of a crime scene. One way to do that is to make an educated guess, and then ask how well the guess explains the observable facts. If you've got a body with a hole in it, and a bullet in the bottom of the hole, it's legitimate to conjecture a gun. The social scientists do the same thing—conjecture an explanation, and then see how well the explanation fits the evidence we do have.

What happens here is that the traditional vocabulary of the Social Sciences turns out to be extremely useful in making these educated guesses. As we work the biblical evidence, we discover certain observable patterns within similar cultural contexts. Then we use these like a grid, and discover that a good many of the loose ends of the biblical text are cleared up in the process.

Contrasting Norms and Variations

One of the observations the social scientists have made is that people tend to record the exception, rather than the rule. I've kept a journal for almost thirty years. I record all sorts of stuff in my journal—where and when I've traveled, conversations, reactions I've had to people and places, even simple descriptions of the landscape. But only two times have I recorded what I had for breakfast—one at a kibbutz on the shore of Galilee named Nof Ginossar, and a second at the Budapest Marriott. I recorded these because they were truly extraordinary. The tables groaned with food. I've never bothered to write down my usual breakfast of grape-fruit, toast, and jelly. Why would I do that?

But the exception is only an exception because it's contrasted with some norm. If I always ate at Nof Ginossar, I wouldn't have noticed the groaning tables. This provides a helpful clue about how to sift the evidence in the Bible: *Something gets written down because it's noticed, and things get noticed when they're exceptions to some norm.* With that clue in hand, we can try this tack: What if we used the inverse of what is written down as a heuristic device to see if we can't get a better explanation of the details?

One of the early Christian historians describes the martyrdom of James the brother of Jesus, then adds this remarkable comment:

> James was so admirable a man and so celebrated among all for his justice, that the more sensible *even of the Jews* were of the opinion that this was the cause of the siege of Jerusalem....

The *historian* would look at this document and study the causal factors that led to James's death. What did his opponents have to gain? Is the source credible, or motivated by some bias or vested interest? What the *social scientist* notices is that many of the Jews objected when James was martyred. That tells us something important: Even though James was a Christian, his piety was entirely acceptable to many of the Jews. This also tells us that James was significant enough that his death was a matter of public notice.

Attending to Social Functions

Now, if the social scientists are interested in the belief systems, and systems of social control, that means that it's not enough to gather facts; we have to ask how those systems actually functioned. In order for a social system to function *as a system*, several things have to be in place:

- There have to be ways the members of the group can resolve conflicts, which requires structures of authority.
- There have to be boundaries between insiders and outsiders, and ways of telling who gets let in and who gets bumped.
- There have to be norms for behavior, and consequences for those who violate the norms.
- There have to be ways of allocating resources, especially when those resources are scarce.
- There have to be ways of managing power.

We call these things *social functions*. Consider the social function of language itself. We listen to people talk, and from their syntax and diction, or maybe from their accents, we can know if they're part of our group or if they're from a different part of the country. One could say that accent and diction serve as rough social boundary markers.

When my daughter Michal Beth went to Stanford University, she discovered that the students there have a kind of shorthand way of talking about the various locations on campus. The coffee shop is the *CoHo*, and the lovely Memorial Church at the center of the campus is called the *MemChu*. Youth groups do this too. Almost every youth group I know has a special little dialect they speak among themselves.

Those tiny dialects make little fences between insiders and outsiders. Insiders can see the fences, and outsiders can't. (If we adults try picking up the dialect, the kids will change it out from under us, but they won't tell us! Then they laugh at us behind our backs.) The small-group dialect functions as a social boundary marker. Let's state that more forcefully: Such a boundary marker is part of what makes it possible for there to be a group in the first place. In the same way, the vocabulary of early Christianity provided a boundary marker between insiders and outsiders, and was itself a factor in helping the church to survive.

Attending to the Rhetorical Assumptions of the Argument

Another strategy is to listen to the assumptions that underlay the arguments of the text.

Once I heard Marva Dawn tell a short story about a postmodernist philosopher. It seems the postmodernist was invited to address an Evangelical camp meeting, which of course surprised and delighted him.

He was even more surprised and delighted when the organizers told him they had come to share his view that all truth was relative. Then they said that just before his speech they planned to prove that that was so by shoving him from the top of a twenty-story building. This comment had the audience howling. But notice this: Marva Dawn knew that this would have the audience howling. She played the assumptions of her audience like a piano. She did this to make her point, but also to score the laugh with the crowd.

Social Science and the Exegesis of the Scripture

So what difference does this make? In the most general sense, Social Science research can tell us a lot about what early Christianity was like, how it did business, how it made decisions, what it meant to become a member, how authority played out in the life of the group. That's important stuff because it helps us pinpoint how and why the NT books were written.

The social norms can also help us fill in gaps in cultural information. They supply the background information necessary for the arguments to work.

Finally, they provide a way to create emphasis. This works just like other cultural information: *Violations of norms call attention to themselves*.

The Law of Limited Good

Let's consider a couple of examples. One of the observable norms for the ancient world is called the Law of Limited Good: *Everything's limited*. The way the ancients saw it, there's a limited amount of water, limited money, limited food, limited sidewalk space for skateboarding. (VERY limited skateboarding, even. All right, so they never heard of skateboarding.)

So far so good. We can understand that. What gets a little freaky is that the way the ancient mind saw it, the *intangible* things were limited too. There's a limited amount of honor and a limited amount of love (how many of us believe that, even now?). There's a limited amount of Truth, Justice, and the American Way. (According to this kind of thinking, if we want to share democracy with the Middle East, we'd have to give up a little at home to do that.)

You can see how this creates a certain climate of possessiveness, a kind of "me and my family against the world" attitude. Because everything's limited, if somebody "takes" honor from you, you have to take it back. But families have to work together, so the Law of Limited Good leads to interesting coalitions. An old saying sums it up this way: "Me and my family against our neighborhood. Our neighborhood against the rest of the city. Our city against the province. Our province against the kingdom. Our kingdom against the world."

On the other hand, we have to have a way of keeping the "taking" in check, so we work out a counterbalancing rule: The honorable man doesn't take more of anything than he and his family need. To take more than you need is a form of theft. This means the rich don't just get rich by good management; getting rich is a form of thievery. The honorable person who has a little excess—like the farmer who has a bumper crop in Luke 12:13-21—is supposed to spread it around, share it with the neighbors. Next time you read that passage, notice that Jesus doesn't commend the farmer for stashing his extra wheat. He blasts him to kingdom come!

Honor and Shame

Here's another example: in the ancient world, the single most important thing a person had was honor. Dishonored people are automatically in a precarious social position because nobody will do business with them. That's why if somebody takes honor from you, you have no choice but to take the honor back. But there's a strict set of rules you have to follow to get it back properly, depending on whether the honor-challenge is from an equal, a superior, or somebody lower on the food chain.

Once, when my wife and I were engaged, I was faced with an honor challenge from her former boyfriend. It happened like this: Shaleen had saved some money for a long-needed vacation with friends. I encouraged her to go ahead and do that, so they flew off to Hawaii for a couple of weeks. A good time was had by all. Her former boyfriend interpreted her trip as second thoughts about marrying me, so he was there at the airport to sweep her off her feet when she got home. This was a challenge to my honor. (I don't really blame him though. I might have done the same thing.) How to respond? I could have beat his pea-brains in, but I didn't. (Actually, he could have beaten mine in, hands down.) I ignored him. By ignoring him, I let him know I didn't see him as an equal. Shaleen went home with me.

The concept of honor and shame may help us understand just why Jesus ran into problems with the authorities of his day. Here's a question: Where did Jesus sleep? The scripture doesn't really say, so we have to default to the norm for the Galilee. I used to think of him sort of camping out among the olive trees, but from the discipline of backgrounds I learned that that's not normally how things worked. In Luke 9:4, Jesus tells his disciples that when they enter a village, they should stay with the first person who invites them, and not move to a better house if somebody higher up on the social scale invites them afterward. Why this instruction? Because if you change houses, you dishonor your original host. Now, if he had this requirement for his disciples, surely it was a rule he observed himself: Stay with the first person who invites you, *even if that person is a lowlife.*

Imagine you're a rabbi in a small Galilean village. A famous traveling holy man and his entourage have entered the village. Word spreads like wildfire. It would certainly be impressive if he stayed at your house. Would bring a lot of honor under your roof. But what's this? He walks right past your house and goes down the street to party with the village's moral idiots. Face it, you've been snubbed. And let's not pretend that the rest of the village doesn't notice; oh, no.

A public snub is an insult, an honor-challenge. Since there's a limited amount of honor, the authorities have to take it back. So we find them grumbling in their beards: "This man receives sinners and eats with them" (Luke 15:2).

Luke leaves us with some gap-filling to do. The Pharisees and scribes are outside the house. In order to address them, Jesus has to leave the party and go out into the street. Now imagine you're one of the lowlifes at the party. When the guest of honor goes outside to deal with some Pharisees, are you going to stay inside and wonder what happens? Not hardly. What you do is get up and follow him out.

So what we have is a street scene, a kind of verbal duel in the presence of a gallery. (A verbal duel is a kind of verbal spat-fest, like the chop-sessions we used to have in junior high school: "Your mama's so fat, when she sits around the house, she sits *around* the house." "At least I got a mama. All you got is a list of suspects.") The parables that follow—the Lost Sheep, the Lost Coin, and the Lost (Prodigal) Son—are told with two audiences. The Pharisees are going to hear the parables one way, the lowlifes another. What they both know is that Jesus absolutely dominates the duel. When the stories are finished, no doubt Jesus turns around and goes back to the party. The stereo cranks up. Everybody has a good laugh.

Except for the Pharisees. They go away muttering in their beards. Jesus has openly dishonored them, and they have to find a way to take the honor back. He hasn't heard the last of this!

So How Do I Find Out More about This Topic?

To my mind, the best introduction to the theory of Social Science research is by my teacher, Howard Clark Kee, *Christian Origins in Sociological Perspective* (Philadelphia: Westminster, 1980). Another, later volume of theory is by John Elliott, *What Is Social-Scientific Criticism?* (Minneapolis: Fortress, 1993). The easiest access to the discoveries made by the social scientists is by Bruce Malina, *The New Testament World: Insights From Cultural Anthropology* (Louisville: Westminster/John Knox Press, 2001), which lays out the material topically, and Malina's *Windows on the World of Jesus: Time Travel to Ancient Judea* (Louisville: Westminster/John Knox, 1993), which is a wacky little book packed with helpful information. More difficult, but still useful, Malina and Richard Rohrbaugh have arranged this material in canonical sequence in *Social Science Commentary on the Synoptic Gospels* (Minneapolis: Fortress, 1992), and *Social Science Commentary on the Gospel of John* (Minneapolis: Fortress, 1998). Finally, note the handbook Malina has co-edited with John Pilch, *Biblical Social Values and Their Meaning: A Handbook* (Peabody, Mass.: Hendrickson, 1993). Apparently 1993 was a productive year for Bruce Malina.

Chapter 11

How We Find Out About Genre

The Discipline of Form Criticism

In the film *Clueless*, Mr. Hall, the homeroom teacher, announces the number of tardies the students will have to work off:

> "Travis Berkenstock, 38 tardies. By far the most tardies in the class. Congratulations."

Travis approaches the podium:

> "This is so unexpected, I, uh, I didn't even have a speech prepared. Uh, but I would like to say this: Tardiness is not something you can do all on your own. Many, many people contributed to my tardiness. Uh, I'd like to thank my parents for never giving me a ride to school, the L.A. city bus driver for taking a chance on an unknown kid, and, uh, last but not least, the wonderful crew at McDonalds for spending hours making those Egg McMuffins, without which I might never be tardy."

I freaked out when I heard this. Why? Because Travis' impromptu speech is a deliberate play on the form, *Academy-Award-Acceptance-Speech*.

An evangelist gets up to preach, but before his sermon he brings greetings from the part of the country where he held his last crusade:

> "It's a joy to be with you here today. I bring choice Christian greetings from the church in Patauqua, where we've been ministering and worshiping with the people of God, and I tell you this morning, there is *Revival!* in the fields of the Lord. I notice in the back there, old Brother Alban, who we worshiped with back in the 40s in the church in Wichita. Ah! and sister Eloise Fischer. I preached brother Fischer's funeral twenty years ago now. It's good to see you, Sister."

Sister Fischer nods and smiles. I frown. This seems to be part of a speech pattern I'll call *Traveling-Evangelist's-Opening-Schtick*. Why did they have to waste our time this way? What's going on here?

Introducing Form Criticism

The answer to that question has occupied the attentions of a group of scholars called *Form Critics*. A shorter definition of *form* could be, "a standardized pattern of discourse." Almost all discourses fall into such patterns. Here's a list of some common forms in English: prayers at Church ("Dear Lord ... thee ... thou ... amen."), conversations with ticket sellers at the movie theatre ("Six for *Robocop*, please. One senior discount." Ouch.), recipes, weather reports, obituaries, sermons, personal letters, jokes.

The important point here is that we read different forms in different ways. Let's look at a couple of examples.

Proverbs

Proverbs are big in some parts of the world—I suspect more so in oral cultures than in literate ones—because they're a handy, memorable way of preserving and passing down the practical wisdom of the community:

- A stitch in time saves nine.
- You can't make a silk purse out of a sow's ear.
- An ant on the move does more than a dozing ox.
- I wept because I had no shoes, until I met a man who had no feet.

We listen to proverbs by connecting them with some current problem, to which they're addressed. Where the proverb came from or who thunk it up isn't really important.

Recipes

Recipes are probably the most recognizable form in any language. Some of the folks at our church put together a recipe book. I contributed a medieval recipe for camel hump, with the note that the trick with camel hump is to use fresh ingredients.

> Cut 4 pounds of camel meat. Mix one pound camel hump and 1 pound camel liver in julienne. Put the meat in a pot with 1 cup water, 1⅓ cups oil, the juice of 1 pound onions, and 11 tablespoons salt. Cook loosely covered, until the water has evaporated and the meat starts to fry. Add 2 cups vinegar and cook until tender. Then throw in the liver with 1 cup onion puree and plenty of coriander, salt, pepper, and caraway. Cook until done.

It's remarkable how stable this form has been over time. In the second century BC, a Roman statesman named Marcus Porcius Cato published a little book of advice for farmers, called *De Agricultura*, or *On Farming*. In that book he provides us with a recipe for cheesecake:

> Grind two pounds of cheese thoroughly in a mortar. After grinding well, add one pound of winter wheat flour, or—for gourmet palates—one half pound of the finest wheat flour, and stir thoroughly with the cheese. Add one egg and stir well. Shape a cake with the mixture and wrap it in leaves. Bake lightly in a warm oven under an earthenware dish.

As old as this recipe is, it seems remarkably up to date. Substitute *aluminum foil* for *leaves*, add details about time and temperature, and this could have come straight from *The Joy of Cooking*.

Implications

Now, these examples and any others we might have cooked up seem to raise some useful questions:

- Why did the form of the recipe remain substantially unchanged all these years?
- Why does the form of a personal letter differ from that of a business letter?
- What role does form play in reading?

These are important questions, and as we answer them we can get a better sense of the importance of form for understanding biblical literature.

The Role of Form in Reading

In reading, form functions in three ways: It focuses the readers' attention in certain directions, it limits the readers' imaginative freedom, and it primes the readers' expectations and so provides a vehicle for emphasis.

Form Limits the Readers' Freedom in Gap-Filling

Different forms permit varying degrees of latitude in filling in gaps. For example, the form *proverb* calls for a different sort of gap-filling than does the form *newspaper report*. The "truth" of a proverb is found as its gaps are filled by reference to the immediate circumstances to which it's applied. My mother threw the proverb about the *stitch in time saving nine* around like a javelin, and it hardly mattered what it hit, it always made sense. The "truth" of a newspaper story is found as its gaps are filled with reference to the historical event that it describes. These two forms call for different strategies of gap-filling, with different ranges of latitude. But *recipes* don't give you much freedom. (Once when my wife was away, my daughter and I decided to surprise her with an apple pie. We learned together that you can't double the temperature and cut the cooking time in half.) These acceptable ranges of latitude have to be learned, just like grammar has to be learned, because the rules differ from culture to culture.

Form Primes the Readers' Expectations

Even before we start to read, we may have some idea what kind of literature we're looking at. I pick up a John Grisham novel, and before I open the cover, I know that it's probably going to be about some technicality of law run amuck. A minister gets up at a wedding, and we're not surprised if she begins, "Dearly beloved ..." Our minds automatically run ahead to, "... we are gathered here today."

These, then, are the first two ways in which form governs reading: It controls the reader's imaginative latitude, and it tells the reader what to expect next, and then next after that. These two aspects of form often work together. Suppose a story begins,

> *Once upon a time*, Frog went to see Toad. They had coffee and donuts by the lake.

We know right away not to object that frogs don't associate with toads, or that neither frogs nor toads drink coffee or eat donuts. That's because the form *fictional story* gives us a lot of freedom. In *fictional stories* the rules of science are suspended. In *newspaper reports* they're not.

Genre Signals

Sometimes we're attuned to form even before we start to read. It's like ordering a steak in a restaurant—we're salivating long before the steak reaches the table. Our expectations are already running ahead of the reading, and those expectations mean that reading has a sense of direction about it even before we start. Show up at a wedding, and you expect a wedding ceremony.

But maybe we got it wrong, so we look for form signals to reassure us and confirm that we're on the right track. These signals are called *genre signals*, and they usually occur quite early in a text. An old man stands in front of a gang of children, and begins, "Once upon a time ...," and we plunge right in and listen for the fairy tale.

If the form begins, "Dear Jerry ..." I know I have to obey a very different set of interpretive rules.

Violations of Form Create Emphasis

But if the form begins, "Dear Jerry—This is the hardest letter I'll ever have to write ..." I know I'm in for grief. It's grief in part because it violates a norm. I'm used to "*Dear Jerry*, ..." My heart sings as I tear open the envelope. Then I get to the bit about this being the hardest letter she'll ever have to write *yada yada yada*, and my heart goes to my shoes.

The letter ended up with *sincerely*, where she used to write *love*. Forty years later, I still bleed from the wound.

Now here's a subtlety: What if the writer plays us? What if he or she subverts the expectations intentionally and gives us something different from what we were expecting? We get a little jazz going on between what we expected and what we ended up with:

A lie is an abomination to the Lord, and an ever present help in time of trouble.

But of course, the subversion can be devastating too. Years ago, my wife and I attended the wedding of a friend. The minister began well enough. ("Dearly beloved, we are gathered here today ...") About halfway in, it became time for the wedding homily. This too is a form. Ordinarily, a *wedding homily* is supposed to be short and sweet, a kind of poem. This minister had a different view. He thought it was about giving advice. Not only that, apparently he had had a fight with his wife that morning. He began well enough. He turned to the groom and said, "Look at her. She's beautiful." A good beginning. We settled in for the poem. Then the minister said, "She'll never be this beautiful again." Things deteriorated from that point. "The day will come when you will regret that you ever saw her. You'll want to hunt me down and shoot me. I guarantee it. And when that day comes ..." The effect on the congregation was electric. We all sat bolt upright and looked at the bride's mother, who was rummaging in her purse for a pistol.

So here's the point: *Violations of the norm call attention to themselves.* (Do we hear a theme developing here?) This marriage occurred more than twenty years ago. We do not remember the names of either the bride or the groom, but we will remember that terrible homily forever. The point here is that if we don't know what the norm is, we're not likely to be recognize the violation of the norm, so whatever emphasis the author intended goes right over our heads.

Some Examples from the New Testament

Here's the problem: Just as other aspects of culture evolve and change over time, so does form. We're constantly inventing new forms, or changing old forms into new shapes. Old forms die out and are replaced by new ones. That means that expectations of form for modern English don't always match those for ancient Greek.

Letter Form

In the ancient world, letters usually had the following parts:

- Name of Writer
- Name of Addressee
- The word "hello," or "greetings"
- A prayer, blessing, or thanksgiving
- The body of the letter
- Closing instructions
- The word "good-bye," or "farewell."

Here's an example:

> Irenaeus to Apollinarius his dearest brother, many greetings.
>
> I pray constantly for your health, and I myself am well.
>
> I wish you to know that I reached land on the sixth of the month of Epeiph and we unloaded our cargo on the eighteenth of the same month. I went up to Rome on the twenty-fifth of the same month and the place welcomed us as the god willed, and we are daily expecting our discharge, it so being that up till today nobody in the corn fleet has been released.
>
> Many salutations to your wife and to Serenus and to all who love you, each by name.
>
> Good-bye.

Most of Paul's letters follow this same pattern, except that they're much longer and therefore more complex. But look at how Paul violates the norm in his Epistle to the Galatians. He begins normally enough:

Name of Writer

Paul an apostle ...

Name of Addressee

To the churches of Galatia,

The word, "hello" (Greek: *chaire*)

Grace (*charis*; notice the play on *chaire!*) to you and peace ...

Then he slips in a shocker. Instead of the Prayer, Blessing, or Thanksgiving, Paul gives them this:

> I am astonished that you are so quickly deserting him who called you in the grace of Christ and turning to a different gospel—not that there is another gospel, but there are some who trouble you and want to pervert the gospel of Christ. But even if we, or an angel from heaven, should preach to you a gospel contrary to that which we preached to you, *let him be accursed*. As we have said before, so now I say again, If any one is preaching to you a gospel contrary to that which you received, *let him be accursed*. (1:6-9, emphasis added)

It's clear enough that Paul was angry when he wrote this letter. What drives the point home for the Galatians is that he subverted their expectation: Where there should have been a blessing, he skewers them with a curse—twice!

Pronouncement Stories

Pronouncement stories are stories in which everything is intended to get the reader to the *pronouncement*, or *aphorism* at the end. (An *aphorism* is a short, pithy saying.) They typically have only two parts:

- The Set-up
- The Aphorism

In a sense, the aphorism controls the content and structure of the pronouncement story the way a punch line controls the content and structure of a joke. We can tell this because pronouncement stories typically quit after the aphorism. Here's an example from Mark 3:31-35:

- **Set-up:**

> And his mother and his brothers came; and standing outside they sent to him and called him. And a crowd was sitting about him; and they said to him, *"Your mother and your brothers are outside, asking for you."* And he replied, *"Who are my mother and my brothers?"* And looking around on those who sat about him, he said, *"Here are my mother and my brothers!*

• **Aphorism**

> *Whoever does the will of God is my brother, and sister, and mother."*

After the aphorism, the story just quits. I may really really want to know how Jesus' mom and siblings reacted to such a comment. (I imagine they're freaked by it; they're already ticked at him. Check out v. 21.) I'd really like to know where this took place. Mark didn't seem to care about any of that. What we do know is that—whatever else we may make of the story—Mark considered the aphorism to be its point, and so he subordinated everything else to that.

There Are Lots of Forms in the Bible That Are No Longer Commonly Understood

We could go on here for some time because there are hundreds of forms in the Bible, and most of them are strange to us: *darash* consultations, miracles, exorcisms, apocalypses, suzerain-vassal treaties, psalms, laments, hymns and other confessional statements, chiasms, theophanies, testaments. Because we're not used to reading these forms, we're likely to think they're unimportant. But let's pause a moment and think about that. What if the tables were turned? What if they were reading our stuff and discounted our forms? Wouldn't it be likely that they'd miss something? What if I tell a joke and somebody thinks I'm serious? What if I write an editorial piece in the local newspaper and somebody reads it as a bare, factual news story?

There's More to Form Criticism Than This

In this chapter, I've tied the discipline of Form Criticism to the skills of reading, but experts in this discipline think forms can tell us other things as well. The question is, can subtle variations of form provide clues to the social pressures that shaped early Christianity, and if so, can we reverse engineer the forms to get to earlier strata of the tradition?

In the mountains near my home there's a ranch complex that used to belong to a famous actress named Helen Modjeska. In her own day, Ms. Modjeska was as famous as Tom Cruise is in ours. She had this place up in the hills, a getaway. There's a story that the ranch originally had a cabin, but eventually she had a ranch house built so she could take friends. For years, folks poked around there looking for evidence of the cabin—an old chimney or the remains of a cement foundation—but nothing was ever found.

Then one day the Modjeska ranch was deeded to the State of California as a historical site. Park rangers set about to renovate the ranch house, and what did they find inside its walls but the cabin! She had had the cabin walls covered over with clapboards so it could be integrated into the structure of the new house, and it had completely disappeared.

Now, suppose that when we strip away the clapboards, we discover that one of the cabin's original windows has been bricked up, and a new window had been punched in the wall several feet to the right. We step outside again and notice that the window has been moved to create symmetry with the newer portion of the house, which has its windows spaced evenly along the south façade. This gives us clues about the cabin, but also clues about the intention of the architect who designed the newer house.

This is essentially what the Form Critics do with the biblical literature. They work at stripping away the outside layers of a story in order to get down to the earlier layers, and at the same time ask how and why the outer layers were designed the way they were. In this way, they hope to reconstruct the historical, theological, and social pressures that shaped Early Christianity.

Some scholars and theologians reject this process flat out because it seems to imply that the stories aren't reliable in the form in which we find them. My own hesitation here has a more practical basis: In order to get to the cabin the park rangers had to destroy the house. If our intention is to read the Bible in the way the authors intended, this will never do. But this is subtle, so we have to think about it carefully. Perhaps the information the Form Critics uncover in their work may add additional data to our understanding of the background assumed by the author.

Whatever else, what we've learned in this chapter tells us that form is important in natural reading, and that if we ignore it we may end up missing something important. So *for purposes of reading* I suggest that we learn what we can from what the Form Critics can tell us about the genres, and also consider very carefully what they might tell us about earlier strata of the tradition and about early Christianity.

So How Do I Find Out More about This Topic?

So in the end, knowing about forms is necessary, and not optional. It's outside knowledge that we can't simply derive from the information within the text. How do we find this stuff out? Here are some resources. One of the best quick introductions to Form Criticism is by Gerhard Lohfink, *The Bible: Now I Get It! A Form-Criticism Handbook* (Garden City, N.Y.: Doubleday, 1979). This is a fun read, filled with practical and interesting examples. It's out of print, but if you can get a copy, start there. Also check out Edgar V. McKnight, *What Is Form Criticism?* (Philadelphia: Fortress, 1969). This book is older and a staid read, but it provides a sound basic introduction to the discipline. A more recent introduction is by Marshall Johnson, *Making Sense of the Bible: Literary Type as an Approach to Understanding* (Grand Rapids: Eerdmans, 2002). Johnson has been lauded for his comprehensive, balanced treatment of the material.

If I were looking for a handy reference tool that described the various forms, I would look to James Bailey, *Literary Forms in the New Testament* (Louisville: John Knox Press, 1992).

Finally, Thomas Long has written a wonderful little book that connects literary form to the task of preaching: *Preaching and the Literary Forms of the Bible* (Philadelphia: Fortress, 1989). Long correctly states that since different forms shape reading in different ways, they also convey meaning in different ways. It follows that preachers can learn from the forms how best to package their sermons.

Chapter 12

HOW WE FIND OUT ABOUT HISTORICAL CONTEXTS

The Discipline of Introduction

W hat we learned about form in chapter 11 suggests that some forms are more dependent on shared personal knowledge, some are dependent on knowledge shared throughout the culture, and others are more dependent on knowledge shared by members of a particular group. Recipes don't depend on very much shared *personal* knowledge, and are more dependent on shared *common* knowledge. They're designed so anybody can pick them up and make sense of them. If my kid sends me an e-mail, she can be really sketchy about what she says because we know each other. A formal letter from the IRS is a whole other story.

This chapter looks at that "shared personal information" stuff. The discipline that deals with that is called *Introduction*. Right away there's a problem: The word *introduction* makes you think, "for beginners," like "Cooking 101." In biblical scholarship, *introduction* is meant more in the sense of *preliminary*. Here's a definition from one of the standard introductions, by Werner Georg Kümmel: "The scholarly discipline of introduction to the NT is concerned with the historical questions of the origin and collecting of the NT writings, and of the textual tradition of both the writings and the collection."[1]

Provenance, Canon, Text

Notice that this definition includes several components. By *origin*, Kümmel means where and when the books were written, why they were written, to whom, and by whom. These concerns, taken together, are called the text's *provenance*. Introduction is also concerned with the collection of the books into a canon of scripture, and then with the transmission of the books by hand copying. (Thus the discipline of Textual Criticism we discussed in chapter 4 is a subdiscipline of Introduction.)

Rules of Evidence

Notice also that this discipline is a rigorously historical discipline. That means that it has to observe *rules of evidence* and *research protocols*. In all there are five basic rules about how we do that:

- *Rule 1:* Interpretations must be compatible with the laws of the nature as they are understood and interpreted by science.
- *Rule 2:* Similar evidence should be interpreted in similar ways. This is what allows us to supply missing data in historical evidence. Sometimes this rule is called the *Analogy of History*.
- *Rule 3:* All historical claims must be validated by publicly observable evidence.
- *Rule 4:* When two explanations are offered covering the same set of facts, the explanation that explains the facts with greater precision and scope carries the day.
- *Rule 5:* When two explanations account for the facts with equal precision and equal scope, the simpler of the two carries the day. This rule is sometimes called *Occam's Razor,* or *The Rule of Parsimony.*

We're pretty familiar with rules like this from contemporary court cases. An expert witness gets up to testify. If she tells the jury she knows how the victim died because she saw it in a dream, the judge is likely to throw her out and get another expert witness. We can't allow evidence like that without becoming hopelessly confused, so we limit testimony to the interpretation of observable evidence, understood in a way that is compatible with science.

So far as religious understanding is concerned, there are some limitations to historical research defined this way. For one thing, it generally presents its conclusions in terms of probabilities, rather than certainties; and it discounts miracles as unlikely because miracles and revelations are not easy to account for using the tools of science. At the same time, the rules of evidence cut out a lot of speculation, guesswork, and illogical hocus pocus by moving knowledge into the arena of what can be publicly verified, so we use them anyway.

This discipline is called Introduction because it deals with the stuff you're supposed to examine first, or prior to the study of the text itself. Historical context establishes the cultural and historical setting of the text, and in that way limits and shapes the repertoire of information the reader is expected to bring to the reading. It therefore sets parameters for all the other disciplines. Because it's rigorously historical, this discipline is one of the most detailed and demanding of the disciplines used in the study of the Bible.

Why Study Context?

At first, this sounds like a rather nonsensical question. Everybody knows you need to know about authorship and context. Why even ask? But here's a scenario that Bible professors experience quite often: A student turns in an exegesis paper. The first six pages are about the authorship and date of the book in which the passage is found. The rest of the paper never refers to the conclusions reached in the first section. This tells us something important: The student knows *that* context is important, but doesn't know *why*.

I think there are two reasons for this difficulty. First, most of our informal Bible studies ignore this question, so people haven't been taught to take it seriously. You seldom hear a sermon in which the preacher talks about where the author was when he wrote. In a sermon, everything comes down heavily on how the text *applies*, and the *where-did-it-come-from* question is quietly brushed aside. Second, most Christians know very little about Christian life in the first century, or about the dates of the various books. It's hard to place a text into its historical context if we don't have a good picture of the context in our heads, so we tend just to skip that step.

Context Adds Additional Historical Information to the Reader's Literary Repertoire

Remember our diagram about an author writing a text for a reader?

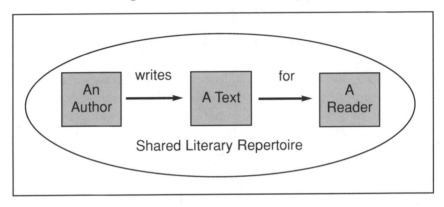

Figure 12.1

But the context in which the evangelists wrote the Gospels is different from the one in which the events of the Gospels take place, so it automatically has a different repertoire:

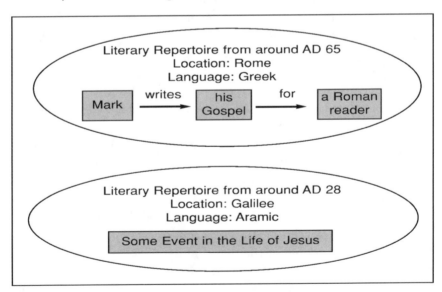

Figure 12.2

All kinds of things happened between AD 28 and the end of the 60s. For this reason, the reader will know stuff the characters inside the story don't know. Indeed, all sorts of historically conditioned knowledge may have become available to the readers because of intervening events, theological controversies, conflict with outsiders, evolving liturgical traditions, and so forth. This additional information is automatically part of the reader's repertoire. For example, if John wrote his Gospel at the end of the century, his readers will know that Jerusalem was destroyed in AD 70. The characters inside the story will not know that.

A useful analogy is the social effect of 9/11. Things changed dramatically as a consequence of that terrible event. What's interesting is that our perceptions of things from prior to 9/11 changed too, in retrospect. Consider the following lyrics from the song "Pride of Man" by Hamilton Camp:

> Turn around, go back down, back the way you came.
>
> Terror is on every side, though the leaders are dismayed.
> And those who put their faith in fire, in fire their faith shall be repaid.
> Oh, God, the Pride of man, broken in the dust again.
>
> Turn around, go back down, back the way you came.
>
> Shout a warning to the nations that the sword of God is raised
> On Babylon that mighty city, rich in treasure, wide in fame,
> It shall cause thy tower to fall and make of thee a pyre of flame
> Oh, God, the Pride of man, broken in the dust again.

This was written in 1960. In the aftermath of the attacks on the World Trade Center, it sounds hauntingly prophetic. In the same way, some of the stories about Jesus seem to shift meaning because their readers can hardly help reading them in the light of historical events that came later.

The destruction of Jerusalem and the temple in AD 70 was a first-century September 11 event. To catch some of that catastrophe, imagine a terrorist crashing a plane filled with Christian ministers and orphans into Saint Peter's Basilica. (Remember what we said in chapter 7 about schemas carrying emotional content?) The events of 9/11 took only a few horrendous hours to unfold. The destruction of Jerusalem took months— it was methodical, it was intentional, it was sanctioned by the most powerful and (to some minds) the most legitimate government in history, and there was nothing anybody could do to stop it. Josephus tells us that Titus systematically crucified the entire population of the city, for which he leveled the forests for a five-mile radius. Imagine Mel Gibson's film multiplied by 40,000. Now, it's unimaginable that first-century Christians, reading the Gospels any time after AD 70 would not know about that event, or that it would fail to shape their understanding of Jesus' story. This is therefore part of the repertoire of information the evangelists expected their readers to bring to the reading.

Let's nuance the diagram one more time by adding blasts for crucial events that the reader will know, but the characters inside the story would not know. Like 9/11, some of those events posed important questions about what God was doing in the world. It was natural and right that early Christians would look to the story of Jesus for answers to such questions. In a sense, they were doing hermeneutics, just as we are.

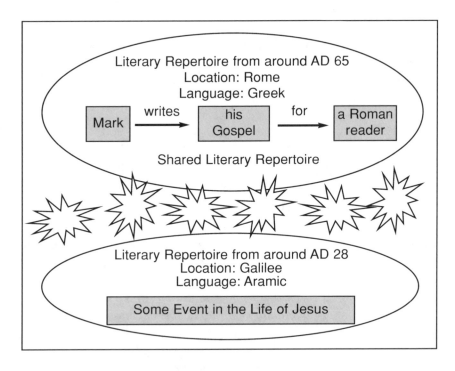

Figure 12.3

Sitz-im-Leben Jesu and *Sitz-im-Leben der Kirche*

What this means is that the story has two different literary repertoires. One is the repertoire assumed within the life of Jesus (the lower oval), which scholars call the *Sitz-im-Leben Jesu*, or *Situation in the Life of Jesus*, and the other is the *Sitz-im-Leben der Kirche* (the upper oval), or *Situation in the Life of the Church*.

Imagine you're a Christian, reading the Gospel of Mark just prior to the destruction of Jerusalem, or perhaps immediately afterwards, and you come across this:

> And as he came out of the temple, one of his disciples said to him, "Look, Teacher, what wonderful stones and what wonderful buildings!" And Jesus said to him, "Do you see these great buildings? There will not be left here one stone upon another, that will not be thrown down." (13:1–2)

You could hardly help but connect these words with the events that were just then unfolding in the Holy Land. It would take your breath away!

Mark 11 acquires a newer meaning, too. Here's the text:

> As they passed by in the morning, they saw the fig tree withered away to its roots. And Peter remembered and said to him, *"Master, look! The fig tree which you cursed has withered."* And Jesus answered them, *"Have faith in God. Truly, I say to you, whoever says to this mountain, 'Be taken up and cast into the sea,' and does not doubt in his heart, but believes that what he says will come to pass, it will be done for him."* (vv. 20-24)

The withering of the fig tree is a pretty shocking story. In its context in Mark, it rounds out the symbolic cleansing of the temple. Jesus is like a Spiritual Health Inspector who doesn't just cite violations of code, he shuts the place down. His words to the fig tree—"May no one ever eat fruit from you again"—in v. 14 are effectively addressed to the temple as well. By the same rhetorical strategy, Peter's words to Jesus in v. 21 are also about the temple: "Master, look! The fig tree which you cursed has withered." Withered, the text says, "to the roots," and thus beyond recovery (v. 20).

Mark then goes on to answer questions that would be ripe in AD 70, forty years after Jesus' death. But how can a person of faith live if there is no temple? Would God still hear one's prayers? How is forgiveness to be found? These are the questions Jesus addresses in vv. 23-25. "Have faith in God," he tells his disciples in v. 22. A paraphrase might get at this idea: "God is not dismayed by the destruction of the temple, so why should God's people be dismayed?" Mark's grammar also permits a different reading. Instead of a command, this may be a statement of fact: "You have the faithfulness of God." Why, then, do you require a temple? The text suggests that—with the faithfulness of God in hand, or with the same faith that God has—the believer too can say to this mountain, "Go throw yourself into the sea" (v. 23). Notice that Jesus has not said, *any* mountain, but *to orei touto*/<u>this</u> *mountain*, that is, the temple mount, the Mount of Zion. So Mark's reader would have understood that Jesus' words here aren't about having faith to cast aside the great obstacles of life, but about having faith to live in direct dependence upon God, without the temple or its practices intervening.

This suggests that in the *Sitz-im-Leben Jesu*, the words mean one thing, but because of the shift of historical context they may come to have a different potency in the *Sitz-im-Leben der Kirche*.

Context Deepens Our Sense of the Humanity of the Text

There's a famous story about the origins of the song "It Is Well with My Soul," which was written by Horatio Spafford, a Christian lawyer in Chicago in the 1870s. Spafford's properties were destroyed in the 1871 Chicago fire, not long after the death of his beloved son. He decided the family needed time away, and arranged to take them to hear the famous preacher D. L. Moody, who was preaching in England. Spafford booked passage aboard the French luxury liner, the *Ville du Havre*, but was himself delayed. His wife, Anna, and four daughters went ahead, and were on board when the *Ville du Havre* was accidentally rammed and sunk at sea. Anna, who survived, wired him the news with this tragic cable: "Saved alone." Spafford set sail at once to join his wife in Europe, and was notified by the captain as they passed the spot where the *Ville du Havre* had gone down and his four daughters had drowned. On a scrap of hotel stationary, he wrote the following poem, which was to become the lyric of one of Christianity's best loved hymns:

> When peace, like a river, attendeth my way,
> When sorrows like sea billows roll;
> Whatever my lot, Thou hast taught me to say,
> It is well, it is well, with my soul.

I loved that song long before I knew why it was written; but when I learned that it had been written in such a whirlpool of loss, it acquired a dimension of depth that leaves me in tears when I sing it.

In the same way, I've always taken comfort from Paul's words in the fifth chapter of Romans. He's arranged his language in a kind of stair-step:

> More than that, we rejoice in our *sufferings*, knowing that
> *suffering* produces *endurance*,
>   and *endurance* produces *character*,
>   and *character* produces *hope*,
>   and *hope* does not disappoint
> us because God's love has been poured into our hearts through the
> Holy Spirit which has been given to us. (5:3-5, emphasis added)

From the discipline of Introduction, I discovered that Paul wrote these words from Corinth, not long after he had experienced something devastating in Ephesus. (Perhaps he had in mind the terrible events surrounding a conflict with the artisans at the temple of Diana; see Acts 19.) Here's how he describes this event in 2 Corinthians, soon after it occurred:

> For we do not want you to be ignorant, brethren, of the affliction we experienced in Asia; for we were so utterly, unbearably crushed that we despaired of life itself. (2 Cor 1:8)

Romans, in turn, was written right after that. Paul's great words are forged in the crucible of real life; when he writes that suffering produces endurance, and endurance character, and character hope, he knows what he's talking about because these claims have proved true in his own experience.

Context Narrows Our Range of Interpretive Options

Here's an important rule: *When we read historical documents, we have to bear in mind that their writers cannot tell the future.* This means that we have to be careful not to read later understandings back into earlier contexts. It is moving and important that when Paul writes, "I have learned, in whatever state I am, to be content" (Phil 4:11), he writes from prison, *and does not know if he will ever be released.* This is important. Suppose some vigilante Christians took the law into their own hands and staged a daring raid on the jail in the middle of that very night, after the letter was sealed and sent. Would that diminish the depth of his claim about being content in his imprisonment? I think not.

Let's work through a couple of illustrations, which I'll throw out a little randomly:

Illustration One: The whole NT was written before the Enlightenment and the Scientific Revolution, so if we want to read the NT books the way their authors intended, we have to set aside what we know about modern inventions and technology, as well as all the stuff we know *because* of modern inventions and technology. We have to forget that the world goes around the sun; and if we personally don't believe in miracles or supernatural beings like demons, we have to set aside our disbelief and read *as though* such things are real.

Illustration Two: So far as we can tell, all of the letters of Paul were completed before the first of the Gospels were written. This means that during Paul's ministry, Christians could not turn to the Gospels for information about Jesus; what they knew about Jesus was what they heard in sermons and stories that circulated orally.

Illustration Three: Most scholars think that Mark wrote before Matthew and Luke. If that's true, Mark cannot have expected his readers to fill out the stories by referring to the other Gospels for more data.

Illustration Four: It's difficult to date, but legend has it that coffee was discovered by an Ethiopian shepherd named Kaldi, in the ninth century. If the legend is right, Jesus' disciples never tasted coffee. (Can't you just imagine Jesus saying something like, "What I wouldn't give for a little Starbuck's right about now;" and the disciples saying, "huh?" and then Jesus saying, "Never mind, guys. Another time, another place." Boy, imagine what the ad men could do with that.)

So the bottom line is that by placing the text in its historical context, we establish an outside limit on the repertoire of background information the reader can be expected to have had in hand: The writer cannot expect his reader to know anything that occurred *after* the date of the writing.

So What Difference Does This Make?

If we arrange Scripture into its historical sequence, and study it that way, we discover a tapestry of understandings being slowly woven. Earlier writers could not have known what was coming down the historical pike. Later writers built on what the earlier writers did as they appropriated their traditions for new and changing circumstances. This suggests that the earlier weavers would not have known how their pieces fit into the overall tapestry. They too were historically conditioned, just as we are. In their experience, the text is a record of powerful and immediate struggles—to find meaning in this invasion or to respond to that injustice or loss.

Who designed the overall tapestry? Christians with a high view of Scripture attribute the overall design to the Holy Spirit. I hold this view. Readers without that conviction attribute it to the human dynamics of people struggling to remain faithful and hopeful in what were sometimes terrible and appalling circumstances. I also hold this view. There's no reason to choose between these two options; the Bible is both. It is the work of Christians who came before us, doing battle with the forces of darkness, death, and loss—*incarnational theology*. And at the same time, it is God speaking to us through this process—the *principle of accommodation* worked out during real-life earthquakes.

A First Criterion for Validity in Reading

The material in chapters 7–12 suggest a first criterion for validity in interpretation:

> The closer we get to the schemas, scripts, and personal information the writer assumed his readers would have, the better our gap-filling will be; and the better our gap-filling, the more valid our reading will be.

But...

Okay. In the past few chapters we've been looking at how an ancient reader would have gone about filling in the gaps in the language of the text, and we've looked at how the various disciplines of study help us find those things out. We've traded hats as we've worked the various paradigms.

At this point, we hit three snags: First, if we stop too soon, we may overlook some cultural or lexical element that the writer thought was important; but second, at some moment we have to stop, and if don't, we end up getting snowballed by data; and third, if we're sloppy we may end up working with the wrong data. The crucial question isn't just,

What's out there?, but rather, *What's important about what's out there?* How do we decide what's important for the reading and what's not? How do we pare away irrelevant stuff? We turn to these important questions in chapter 13.

So How Do I Find Out More about This Topic?

There are basically five different kinds of resources we can use to find out what scholars are saying about matters of Introduction.

Introductions

Introductions are special volumes dedicated exclusively to the careful study of authorship, date, internal problems, and the transmission of the text. They're complicated to read, and quite technical, often the most detailed analytical writing of all the disciplines of biblical studies. They're generally arranged logically, by book, rather than in chronological sequence. A good standard introduction is by Carl Holladay, *A Critical Introduction to the New Testament: Interpreting the Message and Meaning of Jesus Christ* (Nashville: Abingdon Press, 2005). The standard reference for scholars is by Werner Georg Kümmel, *Introduction to the New Testament*. Trans. Howard Clark Kee (Nashville: Abingdon Press, 1996).

Surveys

Surveys cover the same material, but are written in chronological order and use a simpler vocabulary. They often also supply helpful cultural background information. I recommend that you begin with a good survey. One of the best is David Barr, *New Testament Story: An Introduction* (Belmont, Calif.: Wadsworth, 1995).

Introductory Sections of Commentaries

Most commentaries begin with a section of introduction as preparation for a detailed analysis of the text.

Bible Dictionaries

Bible dictionaries cover these topics in alphabetical order. Every working pastor or Bible scholar should have one on his or her desk.

Flyleaf Pages

Many study Bibles contain one or two *flyleaf* pages at the beginning of each biblical book. These are helpful in a jam, but they're often one-sided. That is, they tell what the editor believed, without explaining why and without presenting alternative readings of the evidence.

Chapter 13

How We Disambiguate

Getting to the Gist

A t this point, we're juggling two balls: On the one hand, we're bringing in outside information, and on the other, we're deciding what outside information is important, what's irrelevant, and what's just wrong. We have to have a mechanism for doing this. What's more, without such a mechanism we would have no way of knowing whether a writer was being literal or sarcastic, earnest or cynical. All the wonderful traps and pleasures of language would be destroyed. The play of features on which jokes and ironies depend would somehow play out. In the end, language would lose not only its clarity and economy but also its rhetorical power.

The short answer is this: We work the various primary disciplines individually to collect information, but we work them together to eliminate information. This process is necessary because of one of the primary characteristics of language we discussed in chapter 6: *Language is inherently ambiguous*, and so I call the process of clarifying what's important and what's not, *disambiguating*.

The Six Reading Constraints

Six basic constraints govern and inform the business of disambiguating
—overlapping lexical meanings, syntax, context, genre (or form), paralanguage, and theme. Let's look at each of these in turn.

Overlapping Lexical Meanings

The first constraint is that we *overlap lexical meanings and eliminate the
ones that don't fit.*

Remember that a single word can house several schemas. (The word
run can mean anything from *a stock-market panic*, to *sniffles*, to *something
that ruins nylons.* That's why it's funny when a comedian tells us, "Big
noses run in my family.") As we work our way through a sentence, we lay
the schemas of the words on top of each other and eliminate the ones
that don't work together. The word *green* means one thing when it's followed by the word *house*, another thing when it's followed by the word
beret, something else when it's capitalized and followed by *House Effect.*
This explains why the immediate contexts of prior words in the sentence
can limit the lexical possibilities available for later ones. We'll return to
this a little bit later on. For now, it's enough to note that the sentence,

- Pam went to see John.

instantiates a different picture in the reader's head than does the sentence

- Yoko went to see John.

If we know who *Yoko* is, the name *John* is likely to summon up a schema
for *John Lennon.*

We could diagram this as a matter of overlapping signals:

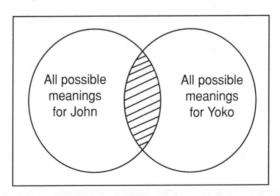

Figure 13.1

We could say that the name Yoko *limits* the options for the name John. The other reading constraints work in a similar way: where they overlap, they limit interpretive options. There's a story in our family that my brother once brought home a report card on which the teacher had written the word, *trying*. That made my parents very happy. They changed their minds later, when the next report card read, *very trying*.

Syntactical Markers

The second constraint is *syntax*. As a rough definition, we could say that *diction* governs the writer's choice of words, while *syntax* governs the grammatical relationships between the words. The cues that signal those relationships are called *syntactical markers*. Consider the following sentence:

• The old dog the footsteps of the young.

This sentence usually requires a second reading. Why? Because when we start, we tend to think the phrase, "the old dog" is about somebody's old hound. But if we do this, the sentence doesn't have a verb, so we have to go back and disambiguate a different way: We use *dog* as the verb, and that makes the adjective *old* into a substantive. This is about old guys making it hard for young guys.

The most obvious syntactical markers are punctuation marks. Compare the following:[1]

> Dear John,
>   I want a man who knows what love is all about. You are generous, kind, thoughtful. People who are not like you admit to being useless and inferior, John. You have ruined me for other men. I yearn for you. I have no feelings whatsoever when we're apart. I can be forever happy. Will you let me be yours?
>   Gloria

Suppose we keep the words and swap out the punctuation:

Dear John,
    I want a man who knows what love is. All about you are generous, kind thoughtful people who are not like you. Admit to being useless and inferior, John. You have ruined me. For other men, I yearn. For you, I have no feelings whatsoever. When we're apart, I can be forever happy. Will you let me be?
Yours,
Gloria

Context

The third reading constraint is *context*. We've encountered context on a local level in our discussion of overlapping and reinforcing lexical meanings. Cognitive scientists tell us that incoming schemas are continually checked against the reader's knowledge of context. It may be helpful to think of context as a kind of target, with larger, more encompassing contexts in the outside rings, and smaller, more immediate contexts in the inside rings.

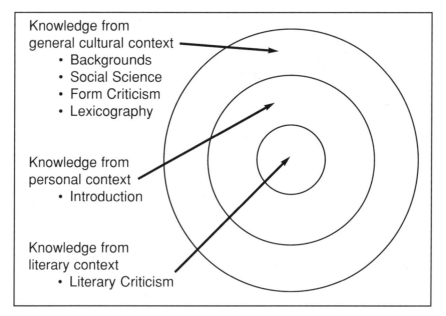

Knowledge from
general cultural context
- Backgrounds
- Social Science
- Form Criticism
- Lexicography

Knowledge from
personal context
- Introduction

Knowledge from
literary context
- Literary Criticism

Figure 13.2

General Cultural Context

The first and most general level of context is the knowledge of the world the reader is expected to have in hand just by virtue of being part of the culture in which the text is written. We learned about cultural contexts in chapters 7–10.

Personal Information Shared between Author and Reader

Sometimes authors and readers share information just by virtue of where they are together in history, their friendship, or the personal knowledge they have of each other. Consider the following sentence:

- I'm having trouble with my old man again.

This can mean any of several things, depending upon where it is uttered and who the speaker is. It would mean one thing from a fifteen-year-old boy on the street corner, another coming from a thirty-five-year-old woman in a Laundromat, and yet another from a fifty-year old man in his pastor's study. We learned about such shared personal information in chapter 12.

Literary Context

On an even smaller plane, context involves the place of a word in a sentence, or a sentence in a paragraph, or a paragraph in a discourse. (Here are some good questions to ask: Why is this word here and not somewhere else? What difference does it make that this passage occurs here, rather than later or earlier?)

It's pretty easy to demonstrate why this is important. Texts are designed to be read in sequence, so the earlier words prepare the reader to hear later words in a particular way. Writers know this and usually provide disambiguating clues earlier. When the disambiguating clues come afterward, the normal protocols of reading are disrupted. The disruption can even be measured. In a 1981 study, Patricia Carpenter and Meredyth Daneman[2] traced the eye fixations of subjects as they read various test examples. Try reading the following paragraph out loud:

> The young man turned his back on the
> rock concert stage and looked across the
> resort lake. Tomorrow was the annual one-
> day fishing contest and fishermen would
> invade the place. So me of the best bass
> guitarists in the country would come to this
> spot. The usual routine of the fishing resort
> would be disrupted by the festivities.

Almost everybody reads *bass* with a short *a*, as in *bass fish*. Daneman and Carpenter showed that the subjects' eyes fixate on the word *bass*, then move on to *guitarists*, then return to the word *bass*, then move back to *guitarists*, then move on. The mental road crew heard all that talk about fishing and set up a detour that sidetracked the possibility that we were talking about music. The reader's mind has to cut across the median to rejoin the flow of traffic.

We can demonstrate the importance of literary context in another way. Try reading the following words:

Rdgnieg. Phaonmneal. Aulaclty. Wouthit.

But if we read them in a paragraph, something different happens:

> *I cdnuolt blveiee taht I cluod aulaclty uesdnatnrd waht I was rdgnieg.*
> *Aoccdrnig to rscheearch at Cmabrigde Uinervtisy, it deosn't mttaer*
> *in waht oredr the ltteers in a wrod are, the olny iprmoatnt tihng is taht*
> *the frist and lsat ltteer be in the rghit pclae. The rset can be a taotl*
> *mses and you can sitll raed it wouthit a porbelm. Tihs is bcuseae the*
> *huamn mnid deos not raed ervey lteter by istlef, but the wrod as a*
> *wlohe. Amzanig huh?*

The point here is that we can only do this by dragging in clues for each word from its immediate context in the sentence. Attention to literary context implies sensitivity to sequence and thus to the linearity of language, to which we will turn in chapter 15.

Genre

A fourth reading constraint is imposed by *genre* or *form*. We learned about genres in chapter 11.

Paralanguage

The fifth constraint is *paralanguage*, by which we mean all of those extra-linguistic clues that accompany and constrain vocabulary and syntax—the modulation of the voice, the tone, texture, rhythm, intensity, and stress. Paralanguage also includes the clues that come in the form of "body language"—gesture, facial expression, eye contact, proximity, and so forth. A shift in tone can signal that the sentence is a question rather than a statement, that the speaker is being sarcastic or ironic, or that the speaker is angry or feeling compassionate, or it can change a sentence from a request into a demand.

Naturally, paralanguage is especially important in speech. It gets truncated or lost when the speech is written down, and that creates a serious problem when we're working with an ancient text. Sometimes there are clues. For example, Luke's story of the anointing of Jesus includes this subtle detail:

> *Then turning toward the woman,* he said to Simon, "Do you see this woman? I entered your house; you gave me no water for my feet ..."

I find it difficult to imagine Jesus raising his voice at Simon if at the same moment he's looking at the woman. The gaze at the woman softens the tone of the rebuke.

Because it's so difficult to recover the paralanguage of the biblical text, we don't cover it in this book. Let's just note that the various signals related to this aspect of language have to be learned, just as vocabulary and grammar have to be learned; so they vary from language to language, culture to culture.

Theme

The final constraint is *theme*. By *theme* we mean the reader's overall grasp of the inner meaning of the story, his or her sense of what the story is about. Often it is the theme that makes the story memorable because it forms a kind of framework within which the details make sense.

The theme is the core of the reader's interpretation. Psychological research has repeatedly demonstrated that the reader's understanding of the theme is a critical element in comprehension and recall. For example, in an experiment conducted by J. D. Bransford and M. K. Johnson, subjects were given the following paragraph, with the title, *Watching a Peace March from the Fortieth Floor*:

> The view was breathtaking. From the window one could see the crowd below. Everything looked extremely small from such a distance, but the colorful costumes could still be seen. Everyone seemed to be moving in one direction in an orderly fashion and there seemed to be little children as well as adults. The landing was gentle and luckily the atmosphere was such that no special suits had to be worn. At first there was a great deal of activity. Later, when the speeches started, the crowd quieted down. The man with the television camera took many shots of the setting and the crowd. Everyone was very friendly and seemed to be glad when the music started.[3]

A second group was given exactly the same paragraph, though with a different title, *A Space Trip to an Inhabited Planet*. For this group, the recall of the sentence about the landing dramatically improved. This experiment and others like it demonstrate quite conclusively that the reader's sense of theme represents a critical facet not only of memory but also—and more important—of comprehension itself.

The tendency to relate the elements of a story to a theme is one of the ways our minds deal with the limits of memory. When we try to remember a story, we may have a hard time recalling all the words. Instead, what we remember is the theme of the story—what we thought the story was about; later, we reconstruct the details by recalling the theme and then reweaving the story by a mixture of verbatim memory, general knowledge, and logical inference based on what is normal.

This has important implications for our understanding of what the original readers of the gospel did when they read. They'd hear a story and condense that into a theme. That theme is what they carried forward as background when they heard the next story, which is also condensed into a theme. Then a third. So it goes. By the time they got to the end of the gospel, they'd have a collection of themes in mind, but they probably wouldn't have had verbatim recall of the exact words of the story.

There is one other important nuance here: Because the themes accumulate in this way, earlier themes suggest what later stories will be about, and in that way nudge the reader's expectations in various directions. Mark 5 contains a series of miracle stories—the Gerasene demoniac story

(vv. 1-20), the healing of the woman with the hemorrhage (vv. 25-34), and the raising of Jairus's daughter (vv. 21-24, 35-43).

When the reader gets to the rejection at Nazareth (in 6:1-6), there isn't any indication that that story is going to be anything different, and the themes of the prior stories are all about miracles. The reader begins the story of the rejection at Nazareth expecting a miracle. But the story doesn't really turn out that way. Instead, it's a kind of anti-climactic reversal of a miracle, which comes to the reader as a shock. Right at the end, Mark tells us that Jesus "could do no mighty work there" (v. 5).

It seems clear that the sequence in which the themes are constructed is an important part of the reader's work. We'll learn about the timed disclosure of information in chapter 15.

Working the Constraints Together

So we're doing two things: *filling in gaps* and *disambiguating*. Both of these activities are rule governed, and both require outside knowledge—the kind of knowledge we learn from the disciplines we've talked about in chapters 7–12.

As we do exegesis, we have to keep these two mental activities constantly in mind. It isn't enough to find out what the individual words mean by themselves, or even added together; we also have to find out how they interact with one another to *limit* the range of meanings in the text, the way the word *Yoko* limits the meaning of the word *John*. This consideration also extends to matters of syntax, context, form, paralanguage, and theme. We could chart this as a Venn diagram: What we're looking for is the meaning that passes muster in all of the various constraints:

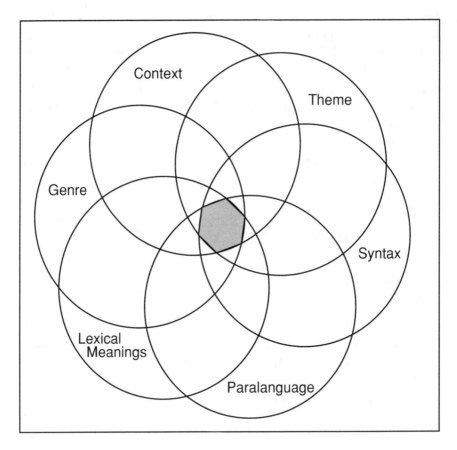

Figure 13.3

When we read something in our native language, we automatically work the constraints together, rather than one after another. That is, we multitask the constraints. Because they operate simultaneously, they can overlap and reinforce one another, working interactively to confirm the reader's decisions about which nodes of information are intended, at the same time eliminating other options. When the constraints are in align-ment, the redundancy of signals creates a kind of coordinated matrix with which the reader can triangle in on the meaning of the individual words.

The key words here are *alignment* and *redundancy*. Let's shift our dia-gram a bit to show that what we're looking for is alignment:

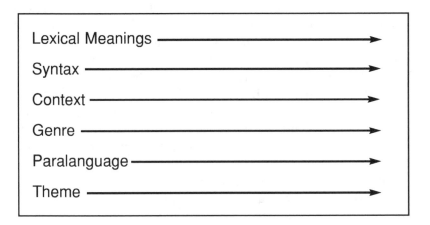

Figure 13.4

When the constraints are in alignment, all the incoming textual signals agree. This produces redundancy of information as the various possibilities overlap. The redundancy permits the reader to make clear and confident decisions about which schemas are intended, which nodes of information are relevant, and which themes to build and carry forward.

A Second Criterion of Validity

Chapter 12 ended with a first criterion for validity in interpretation:

> The closer we get to the schemas, scripts, and personal information the writer assumed his readers would have, the better our gap filling will be, and the better our gap filling, the more valid our reading will be.

The considerations we have discussed in this chapter suggest a second criterion for validity in reading:

> An act of reading is valid to the extent that it eliminates inappropriate background information and zeroes in correctly on the parts of the schemas the author intended.

What we've explored thus far suggests that the mental gymnastics of reading require sometimes dizzying displays of skill—leaps and bounds, layouts, back flips, and cartwheels—as the mind makes its way across the textual floor mat. The operative schemas here are *motion* and *multiplicity*. As it works its way through the text, the mind compares syntax with context, correlates context with the ranges of meaning possible for the various schemas that the text evokes, checks these against cultural and linguistic norms, adjusts for paralanguage, pulls everything into an integrated sense of the theme, anticipates what's coming next, retrogresses to repair faulty understandings.

The interpreting mind is a mind on the move.

Done well, it's a dazzling performance, but the movement creates the possibility of leverage: Sometimes a skillful writer sets the constraints at odds with one another, to trip or trap or entangle the reader. A text can lead the reader in one direction, only to change signals in midair and bring the reader down someplace totally unexpected. The result is rhetorical play, and it leads to a kind of double-exposure effect. In chapter 14 we turn to the matter of polyvalence.

Chapter 14

HOW WE RECOGNIZE POLYVALENCE

Dealing with Double Exposures

L et's begin this chapter with the lyrics of a country song by Dennis Robbins (sung by Garth Brooks), "Two of a Kind, Workin' on a Full House":

> Yes, she's my lady luck
> Hey, I'm her wild card man
> Together we're buildin' up a real hot hand.
> We live out in the country
> Hey, she's my queen of the South
> Yea, we're two of a kind
> Workin' on a full house.[1]

This example illustrates the basis for the third basic protocol of exegesis: *Language is polyvalent.* It strikes the reader on several levels, and those levels often play off one another. Since language is sometimes polyvalent, readers have to have a mechanism for recognizing when this is intentional and for responding appropriately. In this chapter we address the question of how that feat of mental gymnastics is accomplished.

In chapter 13, I said that the activities of reading are governed by the interaction of six different reading constraints. When all the constraints are lined up, the redundancy of information helps us triangle in on what the writer intended. That is, the redundancy helps guide us from what the writer *said* to what the writer *meant.* What we're doing is cross-checking our gap filling against several kinds of questions. In effect, we're asking:

Does this fit the overlapping lexical meanings?

    Nope   → Toss it.

    Yes   → Continue → Does this fit the form?

               Nope → Toss it.

               Yes   → Continue → Does this fit the context?

                       Nope → Toss it.

                       Yes   → Continue ...

As I said in chapter 13, when we read something in our native language, we ask these questions *at the same time;* that is, we multitask them.

In some types of discourse, it is extremely important that the constraints work in harmony this way because the ambiguities of language can be dangerous, and there are moments at which they have to be kept to a minimum. Think how screwy our legal system would be if our laws were written in poetry, or with puns and wordplays as their stock-in-trade. Legal, scientific, and philosophical writing avoids confusion by using technical vocabularies, formal diction, frequent qualifying remarks, and precise attention to form. The cross-checking between overlapping signals minimizes ambiguities, and this cuts out a lot of confusion.

But not all language is technical. When we move to other kinds of language, like poetry and proverbs, things begin to get complicated. Textual signals get tossed around like salad; they create ambiguities, secondary nuances, and multiple possibilities of interpretation. Luis Alonso Schökel points this out in very forceful, clear terms:

> Literary language shows a preference for multiplicity and complexity, it exploits the double personal factor, makes use of connotation, allusion, suggestive ambiguities, it seeks out the unexpected novelty, the surprise, it transposes language to the realm of metaphor, imagination, symbol.[2]

If Schökel is right, we can refine the way we pose the question of this chapter: How do we know when we have left off clear, unambiguous description and taken up "suggestive ambiguity, metaphor, imagination, and symbol"?

Overcoding

Remember how the six reading constraints work in alignment? Our diagram looked like this:

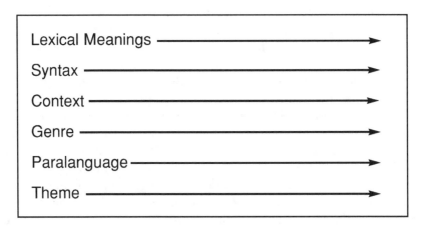

Figure 14.1

Sometimes the constraints point in two directions, like this:

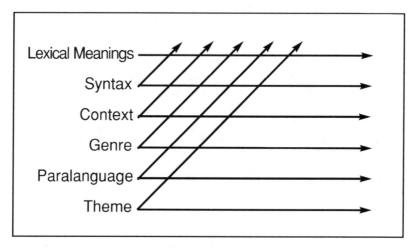

Figure 14.2

The double alignment makes everything more complex. The interplay of conflicting textual signals creates interference, so the mind has to work harder at decoding. A lot of the time, that harder work is physiologically pleasurable, and so we may even experience the conflicting textual signals with a sense of delight. The interference makes our brainpans sizzle.

This is what happened with Dennis Robbins's song about his Lucky Lady. At first, the allusions to card playing appear as secondary nodes of information, slightly below the reader's conscious awareness. If any single line were isolated from the others, the reader would be unlikely to notice the technical language of card playing. When the references to card playing begin to accumulate, they overlap and reinforce one another enough to raise the imagery above the reader's threshold of consciousness. Even though the imagery is brought to consciousness, it isn't sufficient to displace the primary gist of the lyric—a man bragging about his woman. These two gists then stand in conflict, and we play them back and forth upon each other.

I call this activity *overcoding*.[3] One might say that the secondary imagery of a card game is *overcoded* over the top of the primary image of a man and a woman. Overcoding works because the various mental systems for disambiguating—the six reading constraints—function interactively and thus at the same time.[4] The more parallel lines there are that point in the second direction, the more likely the overcode will catch the reader's attention, like this:

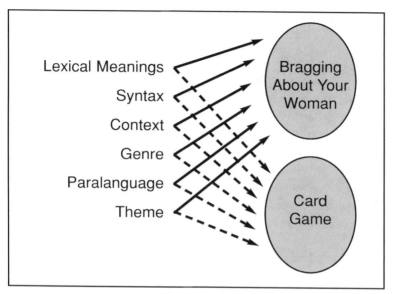

Figure 14.3

This isn't random. The more signals there are that point the reader's attention in a certain direction, the more likely it is that the signals were put there intentionally by the author.

Verbal Interference

The two levels of meaning don't just exist alongside each other. They interfere with each other, creating a kind of mental slippage, and thus dissonance. The mind has to tease out what's really happening, the way it might with an optical illusion. When dissonant verbal signals interfere with one another, the mental gymnastics may call for increased concentration and more intensive effort. This may be why oxymorons and word-plays are so fun to read.

Just yesterday I saw this bumper sticker on a car in the parking lot of an Episcopal Church:

> The Day of Nonjudgment Is Near.

The mind appears to react to interference immediately in one way, slightly later in several other ways. I had to read that bumper sticker a second time to be sure I had gotten it right. So when we see something that's out of whack, our immediate response is to do a double take and check for errors. We can see this cross-checking at work when we have to go back and correct errors of understanding:

- I was afraid of Ali's powerful punch, especially since it had already laid out many tougher men who had bragged that they could handle that much alcohol.[5]

Here, contextual signals ("Ali") prime the reader to target one meaning for the word *punch*, and this appears to be confirmed by the reference to *tougher men* being *laid out*. At the end of the sentence, though, the disambiguating term *alcohol* makes us go back and re-think the meaning of the word *punch*.

When we turn to the biblical literature, the implications are startling. There too, specific nuances of the text are often dictated by the play of ambiguous language, but the cultural information upon which the play depends is buried beneath almost two thousand years of cultural and historical rubble. Sometimes the wordplays are lost in translation, so the natural tendency is to treat the biblical literature as though it's simple, straightforward prose, with all of its signals in alignment. We get a single meaning that seems inherently satisfying, so we quit. The scholars' insistence on exegetical digging very quickly becomes a source of frustration and distress.

But there's a positive side to this difficulty. Once the rubble has been removed, we discover that there is more wit in the Bible than our English translations lead us to believe. In Aramaic, Jesus was sometimes wildly funny; and when he was angry, his wit could be razor-sharp—the sword of his mouth. Sometimes—just often enough—the loss of easy clarity is more than repaid by the exhilaration of discovery and by the realization that Jesus was somehow more warmly human, with a wider range of emotions, and greater prophetic pointedness. Whatever else, Jesus' language shows us someone who was fully in touch with the headaches and heartaches of life.

Wordplay

The idea that Jesus delighted in wordplay was first popularized by Elton Trueblood.[6] Trueblood focused primarily on the dissonances between the subtle and the preposterous that seem to characterize the sayings of Jesus. For example, when Jesus says, "It is easier for a camel to go through the eye of a needle than for a rich man to enter the kingdom of God" (Mark 10:25), the saying juxtaposes largest things and smallest things.[7] The resulting incongruity is perhaps grasped best by Frederick Buechner:

> In desperation the rich are continually tempted to believe that they can solve these problems (happiness, meaning, purpose) ... with their checkbook, which is presumably what led Jesus to remark one day that for a rich man to get to Heaven is about as easy for a Cadillac to get through a revolving door.[8]

Trueblood paid attention only secondarily to the play between culturally coded schemas and wordplays, but these are important too. Sometimes the sounds of one word slam against the sounds of another word. Think for a minute about the background repertoire you need to have to laugh at the meteorologist who names his daughter *Haley*, or the hot-dog vendor who names his son *Frank*.

Speakers of English generally look down on witticisms, especially puns, which are thought to be a "lowbrow" form of humor. (As we sometimes say, a pun is the lowest form of wit, just as a bun is the lowest form of wheat.) But in the ancient Middle East, as in almost all predominantly oral cultures, a rapier wit was a sign of a sharp mind; and the shucking and jiving in the street was a way of managing power. As Halford Luccock has observed, "Humor, like religion, has a way of cutting a pompous strutter down to size.... Humor is a moral banana skin dedicated to the discomfiture of all who take themselves too solemnly."[9]

So you end up with wordplays, like this one from Isaiah 5:7:

> ... and he looked for judgment (*mishpat*)
> behold, oppression (*mispah*)
> For righteousness (*tsedhaqah*)
> But behold, a cry of distress (*tse'aqah'*)

We shouldn't be surprised, then, that Jesus should make puns and wordplays in his efforts to cut the pompous strutters of his own day down to size.

Here's a somewhat complex example. Scattered throughout the Gospels are variations of what are sometimes called "the salt sayings":

- Matthew 5:13: "You are the salt of the earth; but if salt has lost its taste, how shall its saltness be restored? It is no longer good for anything except to be thrown out and trodden under foot by men."
- Mark 9:50: "Salt is good; but if the salt has lost its saltness, how will you season it? Have salt in yourselves, and be at peace with one another."
- Luke 14:34-35: "Salt is good; but if salt has lost its taste, how shall its saltness be restored? It is fit neither for the land nor for the dunghill; men throw it away. He who has ears to hear, let him hear."

The Gospels locate these sayings in various contexts, so it doesn't take much imagination to suppose that Jesus repeated himself, as all story-tellers repeat themselves. The salt sayings may have been part of Jesus' personal collection of "sayings for all occasions." Why would he say this more than once? Probably because it's really witty: The Aramaic word for *salt* is *tabel*. Earth is *tebel*. Drivel = *tapel*. How will you season it? = *tebbelun*. Not fit for seasoning = *le thabbala*. Or for dunging = *le zabbala*. So we end up with a clanging, clattering cacophony of consonants: *tabel . . . tebel . . . tapel . . . tebbelun . . . le thabbala . . . le zabbala.*

It appears that Jesus wasn't just a messiah and prophet, he was also a bit of a poet. No doubt the rhythm and texture of the Jesus sayings contributed to their survival. Imagine the effect Jesus' puns and witticisms would have had on the gallery of onlookers who thronged about him. The lilt in Jesus' language lingered longer in the listener's mind.

Structural Overcodes

Interference also plays a role in a rhetorical effect I call *structural overcodes*. These work by creating a kind of mental double exposure in the back of the reader's head, though their effect is achieved through a different route. Instead of overlaying secondary images by alluding to an existing literary or oral tradition, structural overcodes overlay the secondary images by instantiating a different genre, or the technical vocabulary from a different frame of reference.

We said in chapter 7 that schemas from common knowledge can be evoked in any of three ways. The schema can be named ("icy road"), inherent features can be described ("cars were skidding everywhere"), or technical language can be used ("chains required"). Any one of these strategies can be used to instantiate the range of features that are inherent in the schema, *icy road*. All I have to say is *chains required*, and a picture of driving in the snow pops into the reader's head.

Sometimes, though, the frames can be set at odds, as in this bumper sticker I saw once on a car in California:

CHAINS REQUIRED

WHIPS OPTIONAL

The dissonance creates an oscillating play between primary and secondary frames. In the play, one schema is overcoded on top of the other. The reader is invited to hear both and to let them stand in tension.

Something similar can occur when the reader employs the technical language of one frame of reference within the elaboration of details from a different frame. The resulting play of images can deepen the rhetorical power of the primary frame. A good illustration, though a very subtle one, may be found in Mark's telling of the stilling of the storm (4:35-40). The situation has become desperate. The disciples are at the limits of their strength, and apparently to them, Jesus is even more so. He sleeps on. When they awaken him, he rises from his sleep and addresses the wind: "Peace! Be still!" (v. 39). In English, these are gentle reassuring words: "He whispers to me, 'Peace! Be still.'" But the schemas of Mark's Greek hold nodes of information that are lost completely in English translation. This is the same language Jesus uses for exorcisms.

Consider the effect created by superimposing exorcism language over the top of the story. The language of exorcism gives the story a more frightening aspect, with thundering hints of the demonic. Mark seems to be suggesting that the battle being fought and won here is a supernatural battle, one with cosmic significances. The effect is electric. Mark expects his reader to hear the howling of demons in the background. Could there be a better way to set the reader up for the story of the Gerasene demoniac that comes immediately after?

Irony

Remember that, for the reader, the elements of the story are communicated through the medium of the narration. The characters inside the story cannot hear the narrator at all, and they are completely unaware of the narrator's explanatory asides to the reader. The reader also knows about events that have happened after the life of Jesus, but before the telling of the story. We set this out with a diagram in chapter 12:

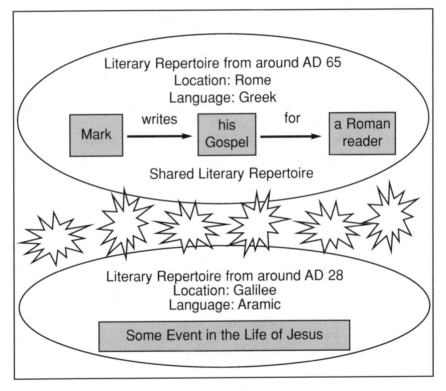

Figure 14.4

The reader therefore always works with a somewhat different repertoire of background information than what is available to the characters inside the story. The distinction between the reader's perceptions and the characters' perceptions brings us to a very different sort of rhetorical dissonance—irony. Irony occurs when the characters mean one thing, but the readers are invited to hear another thing overcoded on top of that.

There are several sorts of irony—tragic irony, comic irony, and so forth—but what they have in common is that they're constructed out of the difference between what the reader knows and what the characters inside the story know. The characters are stuck inside the story the way Mona Lisa is stuck inside her picture frame. Mona Lisa smiles her inscrutable smile, never knowing that outside the frame you and I are wondering what she's smiling at. Without knowing it, a character in the story may drop a double-edged comment, something that can be parsed just as easily in either of two directions, and the narrator may frame the story to give the reader clues to look for the double meaning.

As we saw in chapter 12, sometimes later historical events like the fall of Jerusalem can provide those clues. In John 11:47-52, the Jewish authorities have convened to discuss what to do about Jesus. The situation is politically explosive. Here's how the characters inside the story voice that urgency:

> "What are we to do? For this man performs many signs. If we let him go on thus, every one will believe in him, and the Romans will come and destroy both our holy place and our nation." (vv. 47b-48)

As John's readers hear these words read out in church, they could hardly help but note that Jerusalem had already been destroyed in another way, for a different reason. This makes the political wranglings of the chief priests seem paltry and self-serving.

This same story holds another irony. Caiaphas, who is the high priest (v. 49) offers this politically expedient solution:

> "It is expedient for you that one man should die for the people, and that the whole nation should not perish." (v. 50)

But there are deeper nuances here, and John makes certain that they're clear for the reader by adding an interpretive aside in vv. 51-52:

> He did not say this of his own accord, but being high priest that year he prophesied that Jesus should die for the nation, and not for the nation only, but to gather into one the children of God who are scattered abroad.

So the comment about the death of Jesus is an ironic *double entendre*, on the one level a sly solution to a politically loaded situation, but for John and his readers, a theologically loaded statement about the atonement as well. What makes the *double entendre* sparkle is that Caiaphas prefaces his blind prophecy with these words— *humeis ouk oidate ouden*— "you guys don't know nothing."

The implication for the exegesis of Scripture is clear: If, on the one hand, we read the text only in the light of genre and ignore context and theme, or if we consider only context and ignore theme and genre, we will be unable to detect the conflict of clues that signals the presence of wordplay, irony, and plays on genre. We'll see only the flat picture and miss the verbal double exposure. On the other hand, if we attune our sensitivities more broadly, if we look for redundancy of signals and places where that redundancy is somehow violated, we will discover that the Bible is rich in wit and wisdom, a complex tapestry of human pathos, divine revelation, seething anger, and downright good humor.

The last several chapters have dealt with one or another of the primary features of language: Language has gaps, is ambiguous, is polyvalent. As we've seen, each of these pose special challenges for readers to overcome, and each requires a corresponding configuration of skills: Readers are expected to fill in gaps, disambiguate, and respond to polyvalence.

The essential point here is that challenges for readers create opportunities for writers. Writers know that readers have to work the text in certain ways, and they strategize the presentation of the facts to take advantage of this natural readerly work. They may withhold information, may prime the reader in one direction (thus masking other possibilities), and then bring the reader down somewhere completely unexpected. They may overcode their language with suggestive associations, double entendres, wordplays, and ironies.

Sometimes the polyvalence is created by allusions and echoes to other literature or oral traditions; and when this is intentional, valid exegesis has to take those other traditions into account. In chapter 15 we address the matter of intertextuality.

Chapter 15

HOW WE DEAL WITH INTERTEXTUALITY

Dialogues between Texts

Chapter 14 introduced us to the idea of polyvalence, which is the notion that texts sometimes have multiple levels of stress. In this chapter we deal with an especially important kind of polyvalence: *intertextuality*. This comes from the fact that texts don't come out of a vacuum but instead come out of and interact with other texts in oral or literary traditions.

Old Testament scholar Robert Alter asks us to envision ourselves five hundred years in the future, watching old movies. One particular sort of scene keeps popping up over and over again: Two men stand facing each other in the middle of a dirt main street; the camera focuses on itching trigger fingers lingering near holsters. Women shoo children to safety behind closed doors. Worried onlookers sneak peeks from around wooden store-front corners or from roof-top perches where they can watch in relative safety. In every such scene, one of the men has hyperreflexes—it doesn't matter how many people he is facing down or the state of their readiness, he still can draw his pistol from its holster, aim, and fire before they can touch their guns. His aim is always dead on. Literally.

Now, looking back from the vantage point of five hundred years from now, we might not know that what we're looking at is a form of genre

(Alter calls this a *type-scene*): Shoot-Out-in-the-Old-West. But in one of the films, there's a variation. In this film, "the sheriff has a withered arm and, instead of a six-shooter, he uses a rifle that he carries slung over his back."

What would twenty-sixth century historical scholars make of this final film? Perhaps that it derives from a "different cinematic tradition," Alter suggests. But a twenty-first century reader would know that what we have is the deliberate variation on an existing tradition: "For in this case, we recognize that the convention of the quick-drawing hero is present through its deliberate suppression."[1] What Alter is suggesting is that directors expect their viewers to know about the type-scene of the *Shoot-Out-in-the-Old-West*, and they play upon that knowledge. When its elements are twisted or omitted, the conventions of the type-scene are present in the twisting or the omitting. If we're going to understand what we get in this film, we have to view it in its connection with other films of the same genre. That knowledge is what literary scholars mean when they refer to *intertextuality*. Literary, musical, and cinematic traditions have force and movement, conventions, genre signals, and categories of reference, all of which give dimension and shape to the text or film we're looking at.

This is true in the Bible too. Perhaps the most interesting use of a type-scene is in the story of the woman at the well in John 4. She meets this perfectly interesting stranger, who, uncharacteristically for a Jew, talks to her, asks if she's married. (Why else would he tell her to go call her husband?) Apparently from her response to him—"I have no husband"—she thinks she's fallen into one of those OT type-scene stories we'll call Maiden-Meets-Her-Man-at-the-Well, like we find in Genesis 29 when Rachel meets Jacob. (Here's how to tell a good maiden: Ask her for a drink at the well. If she offers to water your camels too, take her home to meet your mama.) Jesus reads her intent and calls her bluff.[2] ("Yeah, right. You've had five husbands, and the man you're living with isn't your husband.") When she discovers she's been flirting with a prophet, she changes the subject.

Allusions

We can also see intertextual forces at work in the rhetorical play of allusion. Allusions work like other forms of background information, though they do more than simply provide an environment within which the reader can parse sentences confidently. Instead, an allusion accomplishes its effects by calling up a secondary frame of reference and playing that alongside the primary frame, the way Garth Brooks's song about his Lucky Lady tickles the back of the listener's mind with images of card playing.

One of my favorite examples of literary allusion is *The Begatting of the President*, recorded by Orson Welles. Here's this deep, resonating voice, telling the events leading up to the election of Richard Nixon, but with King James English:

• In the beginning, LBJ created the Great Society, and darkness was on the face of the Republicans. . . .

What if we don't know the Bible well enough to recognize the allusion? One day in my study I was reading along in a book by Dinesh D'Souza about political correctness in the American university system, and I came across this rather eloquent allusion to T. S. Eliot's poem "The Love Song of J. Alfred Prufrock":

At the prestige schools, such as those of the Ivy League, impressive domes and arches give off a distinct aroma of old money and tradition. Across the lawns the scholars come and go, talking of Proust and Michelangelo.[3]

In order to recognize the allusion, the reader must already know Eliot's poem. Notice that the parallels between the original and the allusion are quite subtle. They begin at first with only a simple pattern of ordinary words that fall into a recognizable rhythm:

Eliot	**D'Souza**
In *the* room	Across *the* lawns
the women	*the* scholars
come and go,	*come and go,*
talking of	*talking of*
	Proust and
Michelangelo	*Michelangelo*

The opening rhythm introduces the allusion, the reader accesses what he or she knows of the poem, then the reference to Michelangelo nails it down tight. The resulting interference is a kind of verbal double exposure that deepens the punch of the punch line.[4] I laughed outright when I read this.

Now it happens that in my office sat my friend Roger, also reading. He wanted to know what had made me laugh, so I read the passage to him. Roger saw only one level of meaning. Why? He'd never read T. S. Eliot.

We can see something of this overcoding effect in Mark's description of John the Baptist:

> Now John was clothed with camel's hair, with a leather belt around his waist, and he ate locusts and wild honey. (1:6 NRSV)

This description alludes to an OT passage about Elijah the prophet:

2 Kings 1:8a	Mark 1:6
He wore a garment	Now John was clothed
of haircloth	with camel's hair
with a leather belt	*with a leather belt*
around his loins.	*around his* waist.

In Greek, the language is virtually identical, so for Mark's authorial reader the allusion is clear. The narrator has identified the figure in the desert as John the Baptist, but the reader knows from the description that it's also Elijah, heralding the coming of the Messiah.

Let's explore this in terms of the timing involved. We've got two texts—the primary text, which is the one we're reading, and the secondary text, which is the indirect reference of the allusion. The two texts work together to create a kind of verbal double exposure. Interference between the frames prevents their resolution into a unified gist. We could diagram the text and the allusion like this:

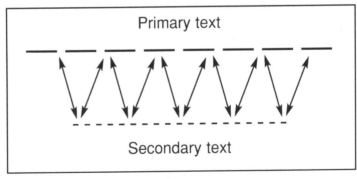

Figure 15.1

The important thing about the allusion is that the reader encounters both primary text and secondary text at the same time. But the reading doesn't slow down, which means that the reader's mind has to speed up to take in the additional information. The mind then scrambles back and forth between the two sets of verbal signals, and as a result, the activities of decoding are automatically made more complex.

On the other hand, if we don't know the passage from 2 Kings, we're likely to miss it the way my friend Roger missed the allusion to T. S. Eliot. Reading flat may be okay. Roger understood perfectly what D'Souza was saying. He got the point, but he missed the fun.

Echoes

Sometimes the connections are clear, but a little more remote. We call these references *echoes*. Consider the following, from Robert Byrne:

> To err is human.
> To purr, feline.

A native speaker of English will easily recognize that the word "purr" was chosen because it rhymes with "err." In the same way, but more subtly, the word "feline" rhymes with the word "divine" from the poem by Alexander Pope that lies behind Byrne's couplet:

> To err is human.
> To forgive, divine.

The allusion and the rhyme are the controlling factors that determined the selection and arrangement of the words in the first place. But they're not obvious. They echo; they don't blast. You have to know Pope's poem to hear them at all.

Quotations

Clearest of all are quotations. Strictly speaking, a quotation doesn't create polyvalence in the same way that allusions and echoes do. In Mark's telling of the triumphal entry there is a subtle but recognizable allusion to Zechariah 9:9. The passage in Zechariah reads like this:

Rejoice greatly, O daughter of Zion!
　　Shout aloud, O daughter of Jerusalem!
Lo, your king comes to you;
　　triumphant and victorious is he,
humble and riding on an ass,
　　on a colt the foal of an ass.

Mark 11:7-10 reads like this:

And they brought the colt to Jesus, and threw their garments on it; and he sat upon it. And many spread their garments on the road, and others spread leafy branches which they had cut from the fields. And those who went before and those who followed cried out, "Hosanna! Blessed is he who comes in the name of the Lord! Blessed be the kingdom of our father David that is coming! Hosanna in the highest!"

That's pretty subtle, and readers who don't know Zechariah are likely to miss it, so when Matthew tells the story he promotes the allusion to a full quote:

This took place to fulfill what was spoken by the prophet, saying,
"Tell the daughter of Zion,
Behold, your king is coming to you,
humble, and mounted on an ass,
and on a colt, the foal of an ass." (21:4-5)

With quotations, the textual signals don't appear simultaneously the way they do in allusions, but instead are encountered one after the other, like this:

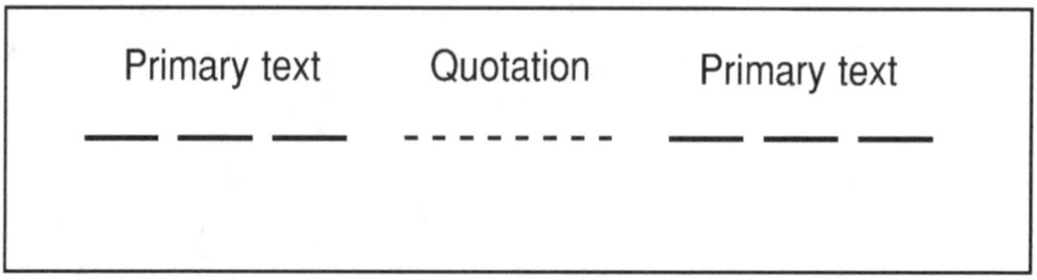

| Primary text | Quotation | Primary text |

Figure 15.2

This takes longer time, and it asks the mind to do a different sort of readerly work. The intertextual reference becomes explicit, but it does so at a cost: The jazz is lost.

But something is gained. In order to recognize an allusion or an echo, you already have to know the secondary literature, the way you had to know Eliot to delight in D'Souza. If you don't, you'll hear only the primary text and not even realize you've missed something. Direct quotations fix that problem because they include even the most uninformed reader. Perhaps that's why Matthew takes such pains to introduce his quotations with introductory comments like, "This happened to fulfill what had been spoken by the prophet."

Intertextual Dialogues

Sometimes the allusions and quotations are intended to challenge or subvert something in the tradition, just as the presence of a rifle subverts the image of the six-shooter in the type-scene, *Shoot-Out-in-the-Old-West*.

Consider the following stanza by Dorothea Day, taken from her poem, "My Captain":

> Out of the light that dazzles me,
> Bright as the sun from pole to pole,
> I thank the God I know to be
> For Christ the conqueror of my soul.

Clearly this is intended as an answer to William Ernest Henley's famous poem "Invictus." Henley wrote first; Day wrote later. Let's set the two poems alongside each other:

"Invictus"	"My Captain"
Out of the night that covers me,	Out of the light that dazzles me,
Black as the Pit from pole to pole,	Bright as the sun from pole to pole,
I thank whatever gods may be	I thank the God I know to be
For my unconquerable soul.	For Christ the conqueror of my soul.

Either poem has its own meaning, but when we read them together we get a little intertextual dialogue going. Day shoves Henley up against a theological wall and doesn't let him down.[5]

Intertextual dialogues can be explicit—in the form of direct quotations—or more subtle, and to my mind more powerful—in the form of allusions and echoes. Either way, they have the effect of slapping the reader down in the middle of an on-going conversation, with two or more texts, rather than just one. As with allusions and echoes, the reader's mind has to speed up to take in the flow of data, which jazzes up the reading process. Day's poem reaches its fullest potential of meaning when we read it in the context of Henley's.

Intertextuality and Common Knowledge

There is a larger sense in which the whole conversation of a culture can be said to function as a "textual" tradition, especially if the culture is primarily oral. Here, too, there may be intertextual dialogues going on. Once I was teaching a course in Costa Rica. The missionary who was my host dropped me off at my digs for the night. "See you later, Alligator," I said. "See you mañana, Iguana," he said in reply.

Intertextuality and Authority

A final comment about a buttressing role played by intertextual references: In a culture that was big on the Hebrew Bible, every reference to the OT deepens the authority of the speaker. It wasn't just important that Jesus could debate with the religious elite of his day. Part of what gives him clout is that he knows his scripture. There are times when he uses scripture like a weapon. "Have you never read . . . ?" he asks his opponents. The crowds cackle and cluck. They cackle because they know that Jesus' language is an open challenge to the honor of the religious authorities. (This is like saying to a Ph.D., "Oh, I forgot. You can't read.") As often as not, his opponents have no answer. The way the NT tells the story, he strips them clean like fresh-caught trout.

So "readerly work" is many-sided. It operates on several levels. Some of the levels are rational and deal with ideas and propositions, while others deal with emotions. What gives the matter coherence is the timing in which this is done. In chapter 16 we turn to the matter of sequence.

184

A Third Criterion for Validity in Reading

In chapters 12 and 13, I suggested first and second criteria for validity in exegesis. The observations in chapters 14 and 15 suggest a third criterion:

> An act of reading is valid to the extent that it recognizes when the constraints of context, genre, theme, syntax, lexical possibilities, and paralanguage get out of alignment. It will also take into account the overcoding created by allusions, metaphors, ironies, and the rhetorical play of mixed forms.

So How Do I Find Out More about This Topic?

Almost all commentaries will call your attention to intertextual references and polyvalence in the text. (If they don't, watch out.) In addition, you may find the following to be useful: D. N. Fewell, ed., *Reading Between Texts: Intertextuality and the Hebrew Bible* (Louisville: Westminster/John Knox, 1992); T. W. Berkley, *From a Broken Covenant to Circumcision of the Heart: Pauline Intertextual Exegesis in Romans 2:17-29* (SBLDS #175; Atlanta: Society for Biblical Literature, 2000); S. Draisma, ed., *Intertextuality in Biblical Writings* (Kampen, Netherlands: Kok, 1989); John Ellington, "Wit and Humor in Bible Translation." *The Bible Translator* 42 (1991): 301-313; Richard B. Hayes, *Echoes of Scripture in the Letters of Paul* (New Haven: Yale University Press, 1989).

Chapter 16

HOW WE DEAL WITH SEQUENCE AND PACE

Aspects of Literary Criticism

W hat we've talked about so far could be set out as a series of steps, or *protocols*. (Remember *protocols*, from chapter 5?)

- Reconstruct the wording of the text using the discipline of Textual Criticism.
- Make a preliminary translation.
- Fill in the gaps in information by drawing upon the research of lexicographers, background scholars, and the social sciences.
- Disambiguate by correlating that information against a matrix of the six basic reading constraints: context, overlapping lexical meanings, syntax, genre, theme, and paralanguage. Set aside facts that are part of the reader's knowledge base, but irrelevant to the reading.
- Where these differ from one another, assess the significance of those conflicts as possible sources of polyvalence, intentional ambiguity, irony, and various structural overcodes like metaphors, allusions, echoes, or wordplays. Notice the sounds of the words in Greek and check if these might be significant.

The result is a pile of notes. This is where we're tempted to quit. It's all so confusing that it creeps us out to think about it.

But here's a reassurance: There's a built-in control mechanism that keeps our brains from getting scrambled—*timing*. We do all this stuff; but when we're reading, we don't do it all at the same time. Timing is the great organizer. Picture a mountain road as it might appear on a map or from a bird's eye view. You can see the whole road all at once. Beginning. Middle. End. Curves and bends. Bridges. Hang gliders off the cliff. But when you're actually reading, you're more like a driver on the road, noticing the vistas one after the other. You take it in a little at a time *in a particular sequence*.

This brings us to the fourth primary feature of language: *Language is linear*. To honor the linear quality of language, we have to take what we've learned from all the various disciplines and transform it into the kind of experience we would have if we were reading the text one word at a time, as though we're on a mountain road, encountering the landscape one curve, one bridge, one vista at a time.

Sequence has a huge effect on the reading process. Consider the gap-filling in the following four sentences, which together form a little story:

> John was on his way to school.
> He was terribly worried about the math lesson.
> He thought he might not be able to control the class again today.
> It was not a normal part of a janitor's job.[1]

Rearrange the lines, and you have a different reading experience. Because language is linear we have to assemble its significances in *the sequence in which they appear in the text*. Earlier stuff nudges us to read later stuff in particular ways.

Real Time and Story Time

The linearity of language means that time passes differently in a story than it does in real life. Suppose you're telling a story about two events that—in reality—happened at the same time. In the story, they have to come one after the other, and you may have to clue in the listener with something like, "Meanwhile, back at the ranch...." This difficulty in timing leads literary scholars to make a distinction between "*real* time"—

which describes the time, sequence, and pace of the actual event—and "*story* time"—which describes the timing, sequence, and pace of the story about the event.[2]

The two sorts of time obey very different rules. *Real* time goes in only one direction and unfolds at a specific pace. *Story* time can start, stop, reverse direction, leave things out, speed up, or slow way down.

(Part of what makes the TV show *24* so interesting is that *Story Time* and *Event Time* coincide, but this is also what makes it unusual. In this instance, the exception proves the rule.)

In "An Occurrence at Owl Creek Bridge," Ambrose Bierce tells the story of the hanging of Peyton Farquhar, a wealthy Alabama farmer during the American Civil War. Farquhar has been caught torching a Yankee-held bridge over Owl Creek. He is to be executed by hanging; the gallows is on the bridge, and he's been tied and forced to stand on the trap, a noose around his neck. The order is given, but when the trap opens, the rope breaks and Farquhar falls through to the water. He manages to untie his hands, then dives deep to escape the shots of the riflemen who are firing at him from the bridge, first random shots, then an organized volley, then a kind of scattershot, then a parting volley from a cannon. He can't catch his breath, and his heart is beating so hard he can hear it in his head. Somehow he manages to escape in the turbulent waters of a downstream rapids. In time he finds his way to the bank of the creek, then onto a road where he makes his way in the dark to his plantation, thirty miles away. He sees his wife waiting for him on the porch, her arms outstretched. This is how the story ends:

> As he is about to clasp her he feels a stunning blow upon the back of the neck; a blinding white light blazes all about him with a sound like the shock of a cannon—then all is darkness and silence! Peyton Farquhar was dead; his body, with a broken neck, swung gently from side to side beneath the timbers of the Owl Creek bridge.

Story time: twenty minutes. *Event time* as Farquhar experiences it: seven or eight hours. *Event time* as it really happened: a split second, less than a heartbeat.

Bierce's story is only a literary fiction, but narrators of real events also manage sequence to heighten or channel the rhetorical effects. There's nothing in the history of the world that says we have to tell the story in the same sequence as the event time. The radio commentator Paul Harvey tells a story about a store clerk who was loading packages into a customer's station wagon when he happened to notice that another customer had left a bundle on the roof of her car. The clerk ran after her, yelling, but she had her window up and couldn't hear him. Just as she pulled out of the parking lot and onto the highway, the bundle slid off the roof, and the clerk rushed out and caught the baby just in time.

Projecting and Retrospecting

What we do, then, is run ahead to make preliminary guesses about where the text is headed, then cut back to fix incorrect guesses. We call these two activities *projection* and *retrospection*.

We project and retrospect continually as we read. We follow along with Peyton Farquhar, hoping, believing—as he does—that he's going to make it. We hear the gunshots from the bank of the creek. We picture his wife, waiting for him on the steps of his plantation house. When we get to the end and discover that the rope didn't break after all, we have to retrospect and correct: What we've experienced is the thoughts pounding in his head in that heartbeat between the moment the trap is dropped and the moment his neck breaks at the end of the rope.

Priming and Masking

Bierce's story achieves its effect by a combination of two psychological phenomena—*priming* and *masking*. We've encountered priming several times before in the course of our study, particularly in the exploration of garden path sentences:

• Cinderella was sad because she could not attend the ball. There were big tears in her brown dress.

When Bierce drops clues that deflect our attention away from what's really happening, he's setting us up for an unexpected reversal.

By priming in one way, rather than another, Bierce also deflects our attention away from other interpretive options. Cognitive scientists call this darker side of priming, *masking*. Since the writer leads and the reader follows, Bierce can lead us into missteps, in this case, false hopes. By manipulating the priming effects, he asks us to identify with Peyton Farquhar, to share his panic and relief, to care about what happens to him. In that way, Bierce sneaks up on us and quietly slips an unnoticed noose around our necks. When the trap drops and Farquhar's neck is broken, we feel somehow that our necks have been broken too.

Masking can take place in a number of directions. We can hold back disambiguating cues or manipulate the reading constraints. Or we can mask possibilities by intruding distractions into the normal flow of thought. Paul Kolers offers the following analogy: A clerk in a store is attending to the needs of his customer when he is interrupted by an announcement over the loudspeaker. The manager has called his name. There's a cleanup on aisle four. When the clerk returns to the customer, he may have difficulty recalling what the customer was looking for.[3] (This is an example of *backward masking*.)

Foreshadowing, Foretelling, Flashback

With the related concepts of priming and masking in hand, we can now make some observations about the way our minds deal with foreshadowing, foretelling, and flashback.

Foreshadowing

Foreshadowing prepares the reader to react to later literary material in particular ways. It's like a reinforcement, only in advance (think of it as *pre-*enforcement). The reader doesn't necessarily know that foreshadowing is taking place, however, because he or she may be completely unaware of upcoming turns in the plot. Instead, the foreshadowing becomes fully potent only when its effects are realized by their later fulfillment.

A good example from the Bible is the way in which Mark's Gospel prepares the reader for the death of Jesus. Everywhere there are clues that the course Jesus is following is going to lead ultimately to disaster. The arrest of John the Baptist in Mark 1:14 may already have suggested overtones of tragedy.[4] The authorities reach the decision to put Jesus to death as early as 3:6. The rejection at Nazareth in 6:1-6 seems to carry that decision forward. Jesus responds with a subtly ambiguous remark in v. 4: "A prophet is not without honor, except in his own country, and among his own kin, and in his own house." When John the Baptist is executed in 6:14-29, the reader is fully primed to hear the horror there as a deepening anticipation of the fate that awaits Jesus. The horror of John's death casts a kind of pall over the narrative as a whole, and when we find Jesus dangling on the machine of his death, the tragedy is deeper because of the pall that still lingers over the narrative landscape.

Foretelling, Foregrounding

Foretelling and *foregrounding* work much like foreshadowing, except that they stand much closer to the surface of the narrative. They may take the form of direct prophecy, placed on the lips of some character in the story, or they may come directly from the narrator. In Greek drama, foretelling was often performed by the chorus, which played the role of narrator and addressed the audience directly.

There are wonderful examples of foretelling in the Gospels. One of my favorites is found in Mark 14. The scene is quite vivid. The Last Supper is over. Jesus and his disciples have left the building and are making their way out to the garden of Gethsemane to spend some time in prayer. On the way, Jesus makes this prophecy: "You will all fall away; for it is written, 'I will strike the shepherd, and the sheep will be scattered' " (14:27).

Peter objects: "Even though they all fall away, I will not" (v. 29).

Jesus' words to Peter are especially vivid and precise: "Truly, I say to you, this very night, before the cock crows twice, you will deny me three times" (v. 30).

Peter is shocked, and stammers out his confession: "If I must die with you, I will not deny you" (v. 31). The story runs ahead to the end of the chapter. In *event* time, these things may have taken several hours to accomplish. In *story* time, they're separated by about six minutes, so the reader comes to the story of Jesus' trial fresh from reading the prophecy of the denial. At the end of the chapter, Mark has arranged two scenes in a kind of sandwich:

A1] Peter's denial begins in v. 54.
   B] The trial of Jesus is told in its entirety in vv. 55-65.
A2] Peter's denial is completed in vv. 66-72.

Because of the sandwich, Mark's readers have the impression that they're "looking through the roof" of both scenes (like a split screen in *24*). The last verse of trial reads like this: "And some began to spit on him, and to cover his face, and to strike him, saying to him, 'Prophesy!' And the guards received him with blows" (14:65).

192

What the authorities cannot see—but Mark's readers *can* see—is that just at that moment, outside in the courtyard, a prophecy of Jesus is coming to pass. The prophecy in vv. 27-31 has primed the reader to respond this way: "How blind they are!" At that moment, the reader has been led to faith on the storyteller's terms.

Intercalations

When one story is housed completely inside another story, the arrangement is called an *intercalation*. (A scholar might say that the trial of Jesus is *intercalated* into the story of Peter's denial.) This happens quite frequently in the Gospel of Mark, in which case we sometimes refer to them informally as *Markan sandwiches*. When this happens, the indications are that the two stories should be read together, their implications allowed to play back and forth between them like Ping-Pong balls.

Here's an example. In Mark, the cleansing of the temple (11:15-20) is intercalated into the story of the withering of the fig tree (vv. 12-14; 20-26). How does this work? The first part of the fig tree story leaves Mark's reader with a number of unresolved questions. There must be more going on here than an act of rage, but what? What does it mean that "it was not the season for figs" in v. 13? If it was not the season for figs, why did Jesus expect to find them? The fact that in the OT the fig tree can be a symbol for Israel deepens these associations. (Polyvalence, remember?) The fig tree story raises these questions, but then stops cold without answering them, so they linger in the reader's mind and bleed over into the reader's interpretation of the cleansing of the temple story. This gives the cleansing of the temple story a particularly stark effect, which is then brought to closure the following day, when the disciples discover that the fig tree has "withered away to its roots" (v. 20). The conclusion is clear: So, too, will the temple.

Inclusio/Inclusion

An *inclusio* (also sometimes called *inclusion*) is a bit like an intercalation, but with a lot more material between the parts. Mark does this, too. For example, he has a large section on the blindness of the disciples, but this is bounded at the beginning and end by stories about blind men being healed, like this:

A¹ 8:22-26   The Twice-Touched Man Who Was Blind
   B 8:27-10:45   Long section on the blindness of the disciples
A² 10:46-52   The Healing of Blind Bartimaeus

Chiasm

Sometimes the repetition is both smaller and more complex. The term for this is *chiasm*: Chiasm is the reverse repetition of several elements, generally within a very small span of text. The word comes from the Greek word *chiadzein*, which means "to arrange in the form of an X," like this:

A¹

  B¹

    C

  B²

A²

Here's an example: On our wedding rings my wife and I had the jeweler inscribe the Hebrew from Song of Solomon 6:3:

I am
  My beloved's
    And
  My beloved
Is mine.

Generally, chiasms stand out in the text the way a poem might if it was stuck in the middle of straight prose. This creates a form of emphasis. For that reason, legal pronouncements and warnings are sometimes phrased in this way. In 1 Corinthians 3:17, Saint Paul offers this chiastic warning against people who mess with his churches:

If any man
  destroys
    God's
      temple,
    God
  will destroy
him.

Entrapment

We've been discussing the elements of timing that contribute to the dynamic movements of the language—priming and masking, foregrounding, foreshadowing and foretelling. Another word for this process is *entrapment*. All of these temporal dimensions of language provide occasion for entrapments and seductions. In a major discussion of reader-response criticism and the Synoptic Gospels, James Resseguie defined entrapment this way:

> Entrapment occurs when a reader is led to make premature conclusions—probably conclusions based on assumptions he already holds—and then is forced to discredit those assumptions and reverse his conclusions.[5]

Clearly Jesus strategized the way he used language. In Luke 22, during the Last Supper, the disciples start wrangling about who's the greatest among them. Jesus asks them this rhetorical question:

> "For which is the greater, one who sits at table, or one who serves? Is it not the one who sits at table?" (v. 27a)

The way the question is worded, it clearly asks for a positive answer—the one who sits at table and gets waited on is greater than the waitstaff. There must have been a pause at this point. Nods all around. Then Jesus drops this bombshell:

> "But I am among you as one who serves." (v. 27b)

So in the opening of the verse, Jesus lays down a rug and asks the disciples to stand on it. Then in the second half, he pulls the rug out from under them, in the process making it only too clear how limited their discipleship really is.

Resseguie claims that "entrapment is rare in the gospels."[6] What he has in view may be the smaller, more focused instances of entrapment, in which the reader is set up and then brought down within a few quick strokes. In a larger sense, however, entrapment may be a fair way of describing the overarching movements of the gospel as a whole. What better way to describe a body of literature that continually leads the reader to a fresh encounter with Christ?

Repetition

Another factor in timing is repetition. In order to understand how this works in the biblical literature, we have to think clearly about what we do when we read a story out loud, and how that differs from reading silently. (In the ancient world, it was normal to read out loud, even when one was reading alone.) When we read something silently, as is the norm in modern reading, we can stop and ponder, or turn back the pages to check that we understood something correctly. When we read out loud, perhaps to a congregation, we can't stop, ponder, or offer asides and explanations. We can pause, but only briefly. Pauses have the effect of focusing the listeners' attention—"Listen closely!" But pauses are fragile. They're like dead air on the radio—if they last too long, the listener tunes to another station.

From a writer's standpoint, the way to deal with this problem is repetition. Introduce some theme, then come back to it later and deal with it again. By doing this, we can clarify and deepen that theme. The Gospel of Mark contains three different predictions of the passion, each one followed by some disciple asking some stupid question that tells the reader they weren't getting it. With the reiteration, Mark creates in the readers' consciousness exactly what he said of the predictions themselves: Jesus "said this plainly" (8:32). The plainer the predictions, the more difficult and obtuse the disciples appear to be. The reader becomes increasingly horrified, not only that Jesus must go to Jerusalem and die, but that his disciples were blind to that fact. In this way, the reiteration of the passion predictions establishes a kind of narrative background for the repeated bumbling of the disciples.

Closure and the Failure of Closure

Sometimes all the loose ends are pulled together and the story ends with a solid thud, like a closing door. The story of Peter's denial ends this way:

And he broke down and wept. (Mark 14:72)

Literary scholars call that thud, *closure*. Closure occurs when all of the various plot complications—the unresolved questions, the foregroundings and anticipations—are brought to resolution.

Not all stories are brought to full closure. (The failure of closure in the first half of the fig tree story is a case in point.) If we think of loose ends as plot complications and tied-up ends as resolutions of plot complications, then it's clear that some stories end with ragged threads hanging out. Sometimes the sense has to be worked out by the reader after the reading is finished. The reader is left with unfinished business. Literary scholars call that stuff *unfinished readerly work*.

Unfinished readerly work explains why some stories get under our skins and make us think more deeply about life. The literary critic Laurence Perrine discusses this rupture of superficiality in terms of "happy" and "unhappy" endings. Literature that is designed merely to entertain will neatly tie off its plot complications, resolving everything into an aesthetically satisfying denouement. Literature that is designed to make us think more deeply will leave us with unfinished readerly work:

> The unhappy ending has a peculiar value for the writer who wishes us to ponder life. The story with a happy ending has been "wrapped up" for us: the reader is sent away feeling pleasantly if vaguely satisfied with the world, and ceases to think about the story searchingly. The unhappy ending, on the other hand, may cause him to brood over the results, to go over the story in his mind, and thus by searching out its implications get more from it.[7]

As I was writing this chapter I asked one of my colleagues at the university if he had ever read Ambrose Bierce's short story "An Occurrence at the Owl Creek Bridge." "Sure," he said. He told me he'd read it in the seventh grade, which was (by my reckoning) over a hundred years ago. Then he repeated the plot sequences nearly perfectly. I wonder why that was?

Sequence and the Reading of the Bible

When it comes to reading the Bible, most of us are pretty lousy about paying attention to the sequence. In my experience, there are three reasons this is so.

The first is that most of us already know the story line, so the surprises are crippled. It's like hearing the same joke over and over and over and over.

The second is that we tend to read the text a little at a time—six or seven verses—just before we go to bed. That breaks up the connections between the parts, so the story is encountered in fragments. Since our minds can't remember all the fragments from night to night, the web of relationships and nuances gets short-circuited and we miss the connections between the parts.

The third reason we miss the plot is that we come to the text looking for a moral or a theological principle, which we take to be the "deeper meaning" of the text. When we find that, we quit. Once I was scheduled to address an adult education class at one of our local churches. The president of the class introduced me this way: "Here's a man who's interested in the biblical story for its own sake; but he isn't interested in the *deeper meaning*." He got the first part right, but the second part missed my intention by a long shot. What sometimes happens is that people suppose that once we get to the deeper meaning—whatever that is—the story itself can be discarded. It's like reaching in a paper bag, taking out the nuggets of deeper truth, then throwing the bag away. To my mind, this is a lower view of scripture, rather than a higher one.

Paying Attention to Sequence

If this is important, how do we learn to pay better attention to sequences? Here are some suggestions.

Read All at Once

One good first step is to read the text all at once, the way you might read a novel. When I was a young professor, I recited the Gospel of Mark for one of my seminary classes, which took about two and one-half hours. When I finished, all 120 students were crying, the entire class. I turned to my wife, who was seated in the front row: "Why are they crying?" I'll never forget her answer: "They've never heard this story before." Think of it! They were seminary students, destined for ministry, and yet none of them, or few of them, had ever heard the gospel story told as a complete narrative. There's an old Taoist saying that a cart is more than the sum of its parts. That's true of the Gospels too. The way we tend to read—a little at a time—is like dismantling a cart and then studying each of the parts without asking how they fit together into a connected whole.

Make an Outline

A second way is to make an outline. Almost all commentaries include outlines, as do many of the printed editions of the Bible, but I recommend that you make your own. The very activity of making an outline makes us pay attention to where the text hangs together and where there are transitions. That act of paying attention is important, an encounter with the text in its own right.

There is, however, a downside to outlines: The authors of the Bible didn't expect their readers to refer to outlines as they read. In fact, the text was usually read out loud, and the congregation was expected to listen; so the building of themes and gists is a cumulative, fluid kind of thing. If we rely too heavily on outlines, they can divert our attention away from the connections that tie the text together. This seems to be one of those places where our tools themselves can get in the way and cripple our work.

So can chapter divisions. Sometimes the chapter divisions disrupt the normal flow of the story-line. For example, the chapter break at 1 Kings 7 disrupts the basic connection between 6:38 and 7:1. First Kings 6:38 says this:

> And in the eleventh year, in the month of Bul, which is the eighth month, the house [of the Lord] was finished in all its parts, and according to all its specifications. He [Solomon] was seven years in building it.

Notice that last sentence: *He was seven years in building it.* This is intended as a set-up for 7:1:

> *Solomon was building his own house thirteen years,* and he finished his entire house.

So the text blasts Solomon, but if we stop at the chapter break we're apt to miss that.

When they're improperly constructed, outlines and chapter breaks can break apart units that the writer intended to be read together, or they can create connections that would be invisible to anyone reading more naturally. Yet they're such obviously helpful tools that it would hardly do simply to skip this step. So what to do? The trick is to make them, use them as compass points, but then refer to them only lightly as we replicate the activities of reading.

Make a Flow of Thought Chart

One suggestion is to find the text on the Web, cut the section with which you're working, and drop it into a Word document. Delete the chapter and verse numbers, then use the word processor to create a kind of *Flow of Thought* chart, that shows subordination by indenting, and parallelism by setting up parallel lines. (From time to time in this book, I've displayed the text this way.)

The point here is that the work of creating the chart is itself a form of observation, so it's important that you make this for yourself, rather than picking one up ready-made.

Practice Bracketing

A final way to get at sequence is a simple trick I call *bracketing*. Remember what we said we're trying to do. We're trying to take what we've learned from all the various disciplines and transform it into the kind of experience we would have if we were reading the text one word at a time, as though we're on a mountain road, encountering the landscape one curve, one bridge, one vista at a time—in a particular sequence.

Here's the trick. It involves a series of steps:

1. Print the text out on a piece of paper, making a line break after each sentence. (A Flow of Thought chart is good for this.)
2. Review the background information the reader is expected to bring to the reading—what I have called the literary repertoire. Your review should include all that cultural and contextual stuff you learned along the way. Pack it in there—don't be shy. What you're trying to do is place yourself in that context—knowing what the author expected his reader to know, believing what the author expected his reader to believe.
2.1. Deliberately *exclude* any information that the author and reader could *not* have known in the historical context in which they wrote.
2.2. Deliberately *include* historical events and developments that took place after the events in the story, but before the story was written down, information the reader would have known from historical and cultural experience.

3. Now, place a second piece of paper over the text, exposing only the first sentence, and ask yourself: Given what the reader knows *so far*, what gist is this sentence asking the reader to construct? What schemas does the text instantiate? Are there allusions to other literature? Social norms? Are the norms violated in some way? What does the text assume the reader knows? How would this pericope be different if this sentence were missing or somewhere else?

4. Move the paper down to expose the next sentence. Ask yourself: What does the reader know *now*? What's the gist *so far*?

5. Repeat.

6. Repeat. Keep repeating until you come to the end of the passage.

Somewhere along the way, you may discover a twist, a plot complication left unresolved, or maybe a challenge or surprise you didn't know would be there. When you get to that point, you are often quite close to the gist of the story as a whole. This is often the story's point.

Implications

Let's summarize this chapter by quoting an eminent literary critic named Menakhem Perry, whose article is entitled "Literary Dynamics: How the Order of a Text Creates its Meanings":

> The nature of a literary work, and even the sum total of its meanings, do not rest on the conclusions reached by the reader at the end-point of the text-continuum. They are not a "sifted," "balanced," and static sum total constituted once the reading is over, when all the relevant material has been laid out before the reader. *The effects of the entire reading process all contribute to the meaning of the work: its surprises; the changes along the way; the process of a gradual, zig-zag-like build-up of meanings, their reinforcement, development, revision and replacement; the relation between expectations aroused at one stage of the text and discoveries actually made in subsequent stages; the process of retrospective re-patterning and even the peculiar survival of meanings which were first constructed and then rejected.*[8]

A Fourth Criterion for Validity in Reading

In the previous chapters of this section, we established a series of criteria for validity in exegesis: Exegesis must fill in gaps with appropriate schemas; must observe appropriate constraints; must recognize puns, allusions, and wordplays. What we have learned in this chapter suggests a fourth and final criterion for validity in reading:

An exegesis is valid to the extent that it takes the sequences of the text seriously, where appropriate excluding any outside information the reader could *not* have known, as well as any upcoming turns that would have been impossible for someone reading naturally. Exegesis is valid to the extent that it integrates such activities into a dynamic, fluid, sequentially appropriate whole.

With this criterion in hand, we are brought round to the point at which this major section of our book began: Interpreting a text is an act of strategy; it involves movement and direction, and both the movement and the direction are important factors in the leverage the author holds over the reader.

In chapter 17 we check out how this process works in practice.

So How Do I Find Out More about This Topic?

A lot of the most creative work in the Literary Criticism of the Bible is done in the OT. Chief among these is Meier Sternberg's magisterial, *The Poetics of Biblical Narrative: Ideological Literature and the Drama of Reading* (Bloomington: Indiana University Press, 1985).

Here are some other places to look: Robert Alter, *The Art of Biblical Narrative* (New York: Basic Books, 1981); Shimon Bar-Efrat, "Literary Modes and Methods in View of 2 Samuel 10–20 and 1 Kings 1–2 [Summary of Dissertation in Hebrew]," *Immanuel* 8 (1978): 19-31, and *Narrative Art in the Bible* (JSOTSS 70; Sheffield: Almond, 1989; reissue: Edinburgh: T&T Clark, 2004).

Readers of the NT will also find helpful: Leland Ryken, *The Literature of the Bible* (Grand Rapids: Zondervan, 1974), *How to Read the Bible as Literature* (Grand Rapids: Zondervan, 1984), *Words of Delight: A Literary Introduction to the Bible* (Grand Rapids: Baker, 1992).

And—finally, but important—Gordon Fee and Douglas Stuart, *How to Read the Bible Book by Book* (Zondervan: Grand Rapids, 2002).

Chapter 17

PULLING IT ALL TOGETHER

Thus far, what we've been doing has pretty much been about taking the text apart and looking for background information. Chapter 16 suggested that when we put it back together we should pay attention to sequence. We do this by "bracketing" the text—by covering it up and exposing one phrase at a time, at each point asking, "What is the reader expected to know *now*? How does that knowledge impact the reading of this phrase? What is the reader expected to do in response?"

But there's a tiny problem with this approach: It's too mechanical. Picture an archivist who works at a Hollywood film studio, carefully examining an old black and white film. In my mind's eye, she's using one of those cool monocles, leaning in close over a light table, examining the frames one at a time. This is, in fact, an important thing to do—for an archivist. But it's not what we do when we see a film in a theater. The individual frames pass before a light one at a time, but the mind blends them together into a fluid, moving picture on the screen. Within the mind, an even higher level of blending takes place, so that we're only tacitly aware of the moving pictures; what really makes our brainpans crackle are the plot sequences, the motivations of characters, the frustrations that occur as the plot complicates, the ironic twists, the tricks and traps. We hiss at the villains and admire the heroes; we learn to care about them, and we may even cry when they bite the dust.

When was the last time you cried when you read a biblical story? When was the last time you were surprised or hung on the plot, not breathing until the complications resolved themselves? Such things only happen when we read fluidly. In this chapter, we pull all of the various skills of exegesis together and take them for a test run.

An Experiment in Exegesis

I've chosen for this example the parable of the good Samaritan in Luke 10:25-37. The story is well known, so I won't repeat it here, but will include it in my detailed comments later.

First, some words about literary context: This is a story within a story. We could diagram this way:

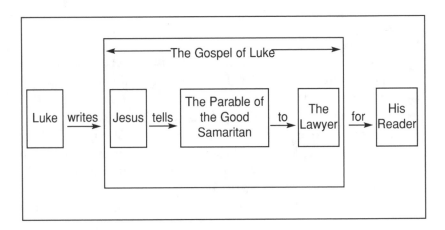

Figure 17.1

What this means is that we have two different "readers" for the parable. One is the lawyer, who is *Jesus'* designated reader (that is, *listener*), *inside* the Gospel of Luke; the other is Luke's reader, *outside* the story. (We'll see in a minute that Jesus is telling the story to two different audiences, who will share some information, but not all.) In what follows, we'll distinguish carefully between these readers, since the readers of Luke's Gospel will have a different repertoire of information for hearing the story. In a sense, they're *overhearing* the conversation between Jesus and the lawyer. We'll turn first to Luke's authorial reader, then cut to the lawyer, then back to Luke's reader.

What Luke's Readers Would Have Heard
Part 1

Verses 25-29

> Just then a lawyer stood up to test Jesus. "Teacher," he said, "what must I do to inherit eternal life?" He said to him, "What is written in the law? What do you read there?" He answered, "You shall love the Lord your God with all your heart, and with all your soul, and with all your strength, and with all our mind; and your neighbor as yourself." And he said to him, "You have given the right answer; do this, and you will live." But wanting to justify himself, he asked Jesus, "And who is my neighbor?" (NRSV)

Luke gives his readers clear clues about how to understand the lawyer's opening question in v. 25: "What must I do to inherit eternal life?" The fact that the man stands up softens the tone of the question, since that's the custom for honoring a respected teacher. But Luke tells us flatly that the lawyer asked the question *"to put [Jesus] to the test,"* which suggests a negative spin, though not necessarily a hostile one. Couple that with the fact that the man is a lawyer—that is, a professional religious scholar[1]— and it's clear that he's not asking for personal advice. What he's doing is testing Jesus' skill with theological questions.

Jesus asks him for his own position—a good strategy in a debate. Get the other guy's position out in the open. The lawyer responds by quoting from Deuteronomy 6:5 and Leviticus 19:18, about loving the Lord God with all your heart, soul, and mind; and loving your neighbor as yourself.

Jesus approves of this answer: "Do this and you will live" (v. 28).

The lawyer's response to this is a little puzzling at first. Luke tells us he "desired to justify himself," which is odd because Jesus has approved of his answer. Why would he need to justify himself? Because rabbinic convictions place theory over practice: How can one properly obey the law unless one first defines its meanings, boundaries, and implications? He's responding to Jesus' practical, "Do this," by leveraging him back into a theoretical discussion. Indeed, the question "Who is my neighbor" was a matter of debate in Judaism. The lawyer is trying to move Jesus back onto his own theoretical turf.

Let's think for a moment about what the lawyer intends by his question, "Who is my neighbor?" Remember that people can't read the future. Part of our problem when we deal with this story is that our own understanding of the term *neighbor* has been shaped by a particular reading of this parable. But when the lawyer asked the question, *he had never heard this parable*. (Another way to say this is that there are nodes of meaning for the schema *neighbor* now that were simply lacking in Jesus' day. For those nodes of meaning we have Jesus and his brilliant parable to thank.)

For the lawyer, everything hinges on a parallelism in the original OT passage he's just quoted, Leviticus 19:18:

> You shall not take vengeance, nor bear any grudge against the
> *sons of your people,*
> but you shall love your
> *neighbor* as yourself: I am the LORD. (NASB)

So the lawyer's question is about race relations: Who is, and who isn't one of the "sons of [our] own people"? How far do the boundaries go? Beyond those boundaries, we don't owe anybody anything.[2] Please notice that no one is subverting the meaning of "neighbor," which is so obvious in English. The English term has largely acquired its meaning from Jesus' parable. The idea of racial or ethnic separation, now so politically incorrect to us, was in Jesus' day quite the norm.[3] (Come to think of it, this is stunningly like the Israeli-Palestinian question today. And the question of Tutsis and Bantus in Rwanda. And Shiites and Sunnis. And Anglos and Hispanics.)

What the Lawyer Heard

Thus far we've been riding along on the coattails of Luke's reader, tracing out the development of the reader's grasp of the context of the story. At this point let's shift focus slightly and look at what the lawyer would have heard in Jesus' response. This takes place within Luke's narrative, like a picture within a frame.

What the lawyer has asked for is a kind of legal ruling, and from the genre signals, it appears at first that Jesus is going to give him one. The opening of the story is just like the opening of legal debates elsewhere.[4] This primes the lawyer to hear the story of the good Samaritan a certain way; he thinks Jesus is offering up an instance of case-law. As we shall see, even though the story begins like a legal case, it ends with a parabolic trap. Part of the entrapment lies in the way Jesus appears at first to be engaging the lawyer on his own terms. We'll examine the details of this shift when we come to them. What Jesus is doing is laying down a rug and inviting the lawyer to stand on it.

Verse 30

> Jesus replied, "A man was going down from Jerusalem to Jericho, and
> fell into the hands of robbers, who stripped him, beat him, and went
> away, leaving him half dead. (NRSV)

Jesus opens the "case" by defining a specific circumstance. The
expression "a man" leaves the case open-ended; to the lawyer, this is
not an actual person but a theoretical one. Note that one "goes down"
from Jerusalem and one "ascends" *to* Jerusalem. These are technical
expressions and have nothing to do with directions on the compass.
The lawyer knows this from his stock of cultural knowledge. The road
described here is well known for its dangers. It descends some 3300 feet
in the space of seventeen quite barren miles. Josephus mentions out-
laws here (*Jewish War*, 4.474), and Strabo says that Pompey routed out-
laws in this area (*Geography*, 16.2.41). This is an ideal place for
banditry. It's isolated and hilly; the folds in the road go deep into the
hillsides, so that travelers are often hidden from view—a perfect situation for a holdup. These facts from the lawyer's stock of cultural knowledge may explain why Jesus refers to an actual road in what appears to
be a hypothetical case.[5]

Yet that realism is masked too. Something about this is stylized. The
man isn't named. He has no face, no identity. He is instead a representa-
tive example. So the impression of a hypothetical case continues, even
though something like this could actually have happened in real time and
real space.

Verses 31-32

> Now by chance a priest was going down that road; and when he saw him
> he passed by on the other side. So likewise a Levite, when he came to
> the place and saw him, passed by on the other side.

It is quite common to find in these two verses echoes of Hosea 6:9-10:

> As robbers lie in wait for someone,
>   so the priests are banded together
> they murder on the road to Shechem,
>   they commit a monstrous crime.
> In the house of Israel I have seen a horrible thing;
>   Ephraim's whoredom is there, Israel is defiled. (NRSV)

To my mind, if there are parallels here, they're too remote to have been detectable. Yet these verses may be of indirect value because they tell us what a lot of people thought of the priests. The negative attitude of Jewish laymen toward priests is widely known, and the lawyer would have brought this in from his repertoire of cultural knowledge. What Hosea 6:9-10 tells us is that this attitude was already voiced within the prophetic tradition.

If the lawyer thinks that Jesus is going to do some cleric bashing, the curt way Jesus describes the action of the priest and the Levite would have reinforced this impression. It's subtle enough in English, but abrupt in Greek. What in English appears as seven words ("he passed by on the other side") is in Greek a single word (*antiparelthen*). That very fact implies a kind of judgment, a dismissal of the action as undeserving of further comment. Notice how stylized Jesus has made the structures of these two opening movements:

> Now by chance a priest was going down that road; and when he saw him,
> > *antiparelthen* (he passed by on the other side).
> So likewise a Levite, when he came to the place and saw him,
> > *antiparelthen* (he passed by on the other side).

But the lawyer is intending to play a debating game with Jesus, so as he listens, he plots his response. He can make either of two moves.

The first move would be to show why it's legal and right for the priest and Levite to pass and leave the man in the ditch. This isn't quite as far-fetched as we might think. J. Duncan M. Derrett has explored this matter in great detail, and we may draw upon his findings with the observation that they represent in a loose way the sort of reasoning processes that are going on in the lawyer's head.

> If the man were still alive the priest must not stand idly by the blood of his "neighbour" (Lev. xix.1). If the priest could be sure he was a neighbour he must make an effort to save his life.... Then the man might die in his proximity, whereupon he would in any case be defiled, which was forbidden (Lev xxi.1); and he would be obliged to procure his burial (provided he were a Jew, which he might well be!); and he would be obliged to rend his garment, which conflicted with his obligation not to destroy valuable things.
>
> If the man were dead, on the other hand, the first two inconveniences would ensue, provided the man were a Jew, unless the priest

confined himself to arranging for the burial and kept his distance. . . . In order to resolve the doubt whether the man was alive or dead the priest must come within four cubits. If he were dead the man would thus be defiled. Poking with a stick would not avoid this . . .

The true positive commandment, Lev. xix.18 and the virtual postive commandment ("not to stand . . .") at Lev. xix.16, were both conditional, and could not overcome the unconditional commandment not to defile. . . .

The priest was thus entitled to pass on.[6]

Something similar is at work for the Levite. What Derrett gives us is a highly developed form of the argument the lawyer would have worked up for his moment of response to Jesus. In Greek, vv. 31f. contain only twenty-six words, so very little time has lapsed within which he can come to such conclusions, so the lawyer's own reasoning processes may have been a bit shallower, but running in the same direction.

The second move would be to point out that Jesus is sidestepping the issue. He's answering a question the lawyer had not asked. The question was where to draw the racial boundaries; but by opening with the negative examples of the priest and the Levite, Jesus seems to be posing a case about the nature of one's responsibilities to a neighbor. In fact, Jesus has left himself open to a challenge that will prove fatal to his position: He has described the man in the ditch as stripped naked and unconscious. There's nothing to indicate whether or not he's Jewish. He might even be a Samaritan! If the man in the ditch is a Samaritan, then he is not a "son of [our] own people," and the priest and the Levite owe him zip. This is the lawyer's second possible move: He could accuse Jesus of waffling.

He has these two responses in hand, but he has to wait for Jesus to conclude the case. Storytelling customarily moves in sets of three. Two examples are too few. Four are too cumbersome. Three is a good balance. So the lawyer waits. As he waits, he anticipates what Jesus will present as the third member of the triad: The apparent cleric-bashing calls for a Jewish layman. The layman will help the victim in the ditch, and the "case" will end up with an anticlerical point.

Verses 33-35

But a Samaritan, while traveling came near him; and when he saw him, he was moved with pity. He went to him and bandaged his wounds, having poured oil and wine on them. Then he put him on his own animal, brought him to an inn, and took care of him.

> The next day he took out two denarii, gave them to the innkeeper, and said, "Take care of him; and when I come back, I will repay you whatever more you spend." (NRSV)

Picture the lawyer holding his question in check: "What if the guy in the ditch is a Samaritan?" He's standing firmly on the rug. Now Jesus pulls it out from under him: "A Samaritan came along ... and helped the guy in the ditch." This is shocking. Several factors intensify the shock. First, the subversion comes quickly, faster than the lawyer can respond. To do this, Jesus abandons the structural parallelism of the first two examples by bringing the term *Samaritan* forward to the opening of the sentence. (In Greek, it's the first word.) The reversal of the pattern creates emphasis. So we get this:

> 31   Now by chance a *priest* ...
> 32   So likewise a *Levite* ...
> 33   A *Samaritan*, while traveling, came near him ...

On another level, the parallels continue to reinforce the contrast with the first two members of the triad. In the rhythmic patterns of vv. 31-34, the repeated *antiparelthen* ("he passed by on the other side") stand in structural balance with both *proselthen* ("he went to him") and *esplanchhisthe* ("he had compassion").

> 31   A priest ... passed by on the other side (*antiparelthen*)
> 32   A Levite ... passed by on the other side (*antiparelthen*)
> 33   A Samaritan ... had compassion ... (*esplanchhisthe*)
> 34   and went to him   (*proselthen*)

Note that *antiparelthen* and *proselthen* share a common root—<u>went</u> *away from*, <u>went</u> *toward*. Jesus is not content to make his point by contrast. He hammers it home:

> But a Samaritan, while traveling came near him; and when he saw him,
>
> • he was moved with pity.
> • He went to him
> • and bandaged his wounds, having poured oil and wine on them.
> • Then he put him on his own animal, brought him to an inn, and took care of him.

- The next day he took out two denarii, gave them to the innkeeper, and said, "Take care of him; and when I come back, I will repay you whatever more you spend."

In the hammering, the story makes two further points. The first of these rests on the surface of the language itself. The lawyer knows all about the dangers of the road and the presence of robbers. All the details of Jesus' description of the Samaritan make him out to be a man with resources. He has provisions for such a circumstance—oil and wine— does he travel regularly? He has pack animals—is he a merchant? He guarantees the costs of the victim's care—does he carry money? Such a man is travel-wise. He'd have to be blind not to know there are bandits in these hills. The beaten-up guy in the ditch is evidence enough of that. The Samaritan has a lot to lose here. His pack animals and his merchandise make him a prime target. He's far from home, in enemy territory. The lawyer knows that the Jericho road is in Judea. The lawyer will also envision the victim in the ditch within one of the folds in the road, rather than out in the open, and thus out of view of other travelers. The Samaritan surely knows that by kneeling beside the victim, he makes himself a sitting duck. And on whose behalf? Everybody knows that here, on this particular road, the body in the ditch is almost certainly a Jew. Against this evolving scenario, the behavior of the priest and Levite appears paltry and self-serving. Since in the back of his mind the lawyer has been formulating an argument in favor of their behavior, it appears he has been tricked into a kind of self-incrimination.

So the Samaritan is portrayed as a hero, a model to be admired and copied. He *defines* what it is to be a neighbor. It's enough to make the lawyer's blood boil. And that's precisely the point. This story makes the lawyer's blood boil. In that way it lays bare the inhumanity of his legal wrangling and shows that he's incapable of providing an adequate answer to the question he has asked, "Who is my neighbor?"

But there's something deeper here: The reason the lawyer cannot properly answer the question is that the way he reads the law is inconsistent with the character of God. The history of Israel reverberates with this central theme: *The character of God is disclosed in acts of compassion.* In this way, Jesus bleeds the lawyer's question of its moral force and reasserts his claim that one must be merciful, not because it's written in some statute, but because God is merciful (see Luke 6:36).

This, then, is the primary organizing theme here. Overcoded on top of it is a second theme, though this one depends upon subtle intertextual competencies. The story Jesus tells has close verbal and conceptual parallels with 2 Chronicles 28:5-15, a story in which Samaritans come to the aid of the Judeans following a battle with Israel. The lawyer would have known this from his own studies. Of special interest is v. 15:

> And the men [Judeans] who have been mentioned by name rose and took the captives, and with the spoil they clothed all that were naked among them; they clothed them, gave them sandals, provided them with food and drink, and anointed them; and carrying all the feeble among them on asses, they brought them to their kinsfolk at Jericho, the city of palm trees. Then they returned to Samaria.

But note the timing: The lawyer only discovers the reference to 2 Chronicles *after* Jesus mentions the Samaritan, and by then it's too late to retreat from the position he has taken. Then the parallels come fast and furious, piling upon themselves, so that the lawyer could hardly miss them. By then it's too late. As with other allusions, this one overcodes a second frame around the story, one that resists resolution into a gist, and that further deepens the lawyer's readerly work. Thus, from the standpoint of reading constraints, J. M. Furness is closest to the truth:

> The Scribe is not answered by a brilliant story invented on the spur of the moment, but more brilliantly and more devastatingly by reference to a tale that the Lawyer already knew very well indeed.[7]

Verses 36-37

> "Which of these three, do you think, was a neighbor to the man who fell into the hands of the robbers?" He said, "The one who showed him mercy." Jesus said to him, "Go and do likewise." (NRSV)

Notice how Jesus appears to have stood the lawyer's question on its head. Here's the lawyer's question (v. 29):

But wanting to justify himself, he asked Jesus, "And who is my neighbor?" Jesus replied with the parable, then asked, in v. 36:

> "Which of these three, do you think, was a neighbor to the man who fell into the hands of the robbers?"

The explanation of this twist in the question may be more subtle than meets the eye. The lawyer's original question may have been ambiguous, especially if this conversation is understood as having taken place in Aramaic. In Aramaic, possession is indicated with the preposition *le*, "to" or "for." To ask, "Who is my neighbor?" is to ask at the same time, "Who is neighbor to me?" In the Aramaic conversation, the lawyer asked only the first question, intending only to find out to whom he was obligated. If this is the case, Jesus has returned to his original strategy and forced the lawyer to find his answer in the question itself. If this is so, however, Luke's reader would have missed it. The text as we have it is written in Greek, and Luke's Greek lacks this particular ambiguity.

Before we leave this discussion, let's review the story in terms of the lawyer's identifications. In vv. 31 and 32, the lawyer is asked to identify with the priest and the Levite, or—at the very least—to take on their case and enter the story from their point of view. We noted that he would likely have expected Jesus to engage in cleric bashing. One response is that Jesus is sidestepping the question. What if the man in a ditch is a Samaritan? When Jesus casts the Samaritan in the role of hero, he disrupts that movement and obliterates the lawyer's response. The final question in v. 36 restates the question from the victim's point of view: Who proved to be neighbor to the man in the ditch? To answer this question, the lawyer must abandon his initial identifications and take on the point of view of the victim, who is *helped* by a Samaritan! Thus, part of the rhetorical power here is the reversal of roles.[8]

What Luke's Readers Would Have Heard
Part 2

With this, our observations return to those of Luke's reader, and we abandon the lawyer's point of view, climb back outside the story, and view it within its frame. In a sense, Luke's readers are allowed to overhear this conversation, though it seems likely that only a very few would have heard the story the way the lawyer would have. That's because the nuances of law and allusion that have overcoded the story in the lawyer's ears aren't common knowledge for Gentile Christians, especially if they're new converts.

But even the new Christian converts know some things the lawyer doesn't know. Remember from chapter 12 that the readers of the Gospels knew about events and controversies that troubled the church after the end of Jesus' life, but before the writing of the gospel? We displayed that with a diagram:

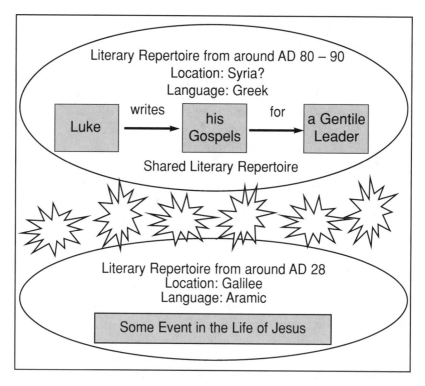

Figure 17.2

One of those controversies, which apparently still divided the church, is the question of the legitimacy of the Gentile mission, and the place of Gentiles in the economy of salvation. In Acts, Luke records for us specific details about that controversy (note Acts 15). More specifically, Luke himself is a Gentile (the only Gentile writer in the New Testament), and this topic appears to be a critical one for him. Indeed, one way to read his other book, Acts, is to see it as a kind of "healing narrative,"[9] designed to bring together these two factions of the church. Much in the Gospel of Luke serves a similar purpose. Luke's reader would have heard this parable as an affirmation of the Gentile mission.

Let's also note that Luke's Gentile readers would not have shared the lawyer's ethnic prejudice against Samaritans, or other non-Jews, or his disposition in favor of the actions of the priest and Levite. (More likely,

Luke's reader would have been disposed against the priest, the Levite, and the lawyer right from the get-go.) Luke has only mentioned lawyers once previously in his Gospel, in 7:29f, but that reference is significant. Jesus has been preaching about John the Baptist, lauding him for his good work. In that context, Luke adds this parenthetical remark, which lumps the lawyers together with the Pharisees:

> When they heard this all the people and the tax collectors justified God, having been baptized with the baptism of John; but *the Pharisees and the lawyers* rejected the purpose of God for themselves, not having been baptized by him.

By connecting the Pharisees and the lawyers together in this way, Luke paints them all with the same brush. For this reason, that whole complex of criticism of the Pharisees is part of the readers' background when they get to the parable of the good Samaritan in Luke 10.

The reader is also likely to have a shallower grasp of Jewish literature than the lawyer has, and for that reason is likely to hear this as a simple story of insiders and outsiders, with—of course—"What must I do to inherit eternal life?" as its dominant theme. Even from the outside, it's clear that the primary stakes are racial. Then, as the story unfolds, even without the lawyer's subtle legal and literary competencies, Luke's reader is bound to realize that Jesus has somehow brilliantly turned the discussion. In cross-examining Jesus, the lawyer has put himself on trial. Jesus concludes by re-stating the lawyer's question:

> "Which of these three, do you think, was a neighbor to the man who fell into the hands of the robbers?"

The lawyer can't even bring himself to say the word *Samaritan*, and the bravado of his opening challenge has been toned down to a whisper: *"The one who showed him mercy."*

Luke's reader sits as a jury of sorts, and when Jesus reiterates in v. 37 what he had said in v. 28—"*Go and do likewise*"—the verdict of the jury is unavoidable.

So Jesus has bested the lawyer at his own game. If Luke's reader is a Gentile Christian who has been the victim of Jewish exclusivism, which seems to be likely, then his or her delight in this exchange would be just as deep as is the lawyer's frustration and disappointment.

To Sum Up

That, in a nutshell, is exegesis. It's basically the same sort of thing we did when we analyzed the bumper sticker, *Toto, I don't think we're in Kansas anymore*, in chapter 6. What made it complicated is the length of the story, the two readers, and the fact that all of the cultural stuff had to be reconstructed from ancient sources.

Chapter 18

LOOKING *AHEAD*, LOOKING *BEYOND*

A Concluding Unacademic Postscript

So we come at last to the end. If much of what we've discovered about the Bible seems strange, even foreign, that's because it is. This is an ancient and often puzzling book, written in another age and a different culture—in truth, several different cultures—and it's packed with subtleties and nuances that are only visible when they're read carefully and thoughtfully in the light of their proper cultural background.

Some people get a little rattled when theologians insist that the Bible has to be read against the right cultural background, or when we say that some readings of the Bible are more valid than others. For the life of me I can't understand why that should freak anybody out. Perhaps it threatens their deepest taken-for-granted ideas about how God works in the world. When I first discovered biblical studies, I found them a relief because so much of what I heard from the pulpit when I was a young man seemed to me to have lost touch with the headaches and heartaches of real life. The characters of scripture were treated in a way that made them not only idealized, but also flat and uninteresting—not *characters* so much as *caricatures*. Some of the most influential people in the churches of my childhood seemed to me to be flat also—good but uninteresting—and they seemed to suggest that the goal of the

Christian life was to be as flat and as tasteless as cardboard. As I've grown, I've come to wonder if perhaps there might be a connection between their flat ideas about the Christian life and the flat way they read the scripture.

Suppose in my reading of the Gospels I miss the wordplays and puns, so I think of Jesus as humorless and dour. Or I think his emotional range fluctuated between milquetoast and mildly insipid, a benevolent and forgiving character, but distant and unmoved by the agonies of real life. And suppose that at the same time, I adopt as my strategy for ethical reflection the famous acronym WWJD—What Would Jesus Do? Wouldn't my insipid picture of Jesus lead me to believe that God wants me to be insipid too? When I sing the old hymn "To Be Like Jesus," wouldn't I imagine that being like Jesus means being bland?

But by contrast, suppose I picked up that Jesus was hugely funny, and that at times his wit cut like a knife. Suppose I noticed that he knew how to party. Or suppose I paid attention to the enormous dangers involved in his confrontations with the authorities. In a famous passage, Thomas Howard describes Jesus this way:

> For in the figure of Jesus the Christ there is something that escapes us. He has been the subject of the greatest efforts at systematization in the history of man. But anyone who has ever tried this has had, in the end, to admit that the seams keep bursting. He sooner or later discovers that he is in touch, not with a pale Galilean, but with a towering, and furious figure who will not be managed.[1]

Would that not lead me and my WWJD philosophy into a spiritual journey that was infinitely more daring? I discovered this, to my relief, when I learned how to do exegesis. I also discovered a faith that is more deeply and richly human—not less demanding, but more so, and demanding in a different way than I had thought. I'm grateful to my teachers who helped make this transition a time of discovery and joy. Phew. What a relief.

Some Reassurances . . .

If you still find it hard, in this closing chapter I want to offer some reassurances.

First, Nobody Decided to Make This Complicated

What I've been doing is describing something that is inherently complicated. I'm reminded of a story about a man who needed to repair some damaged plumbing in his house. He drew a diagram of what he wanted to do, took it to the local hardware store, and showed it to the clerk. The clerk's response fits our situation perfectly:

> What you're trying to do defies the laws of bathroom physics. You're asking that water flow uphill, and there's no plumbing mechanism that can make water do that. The better approach is to learn what can and can't be done with plumbing and then design your bathroom around that.

This is like that. We start with what is, then build our model to match that, rather than insisting that it be something different or we won't try. Lots of important things are complicated. The MR2 in my driveway is complicated. The sooner we get over it, the sooner we can get on with our work.

Second, You Already Know How to Do a Lot of This Stuff

You do it all the time in English. You're just not aware that you're doing it because it takes place in the back of your mind, where you're not looking. The problem isn't with the activities of reading, but with the differences in language and culture between *here and now* and *there and then*. The historical research is necessary because of these differences, but exegesis itself is pretty much the same as ordinary reading. You're already halfway home.

Third, It's Worth the Time and Effort

In a sense, we make a bargain: We'll give x hours to study, and in return for those hours we get a solid, responsible reading of the text. If we do this work carefully and thoughtfully, we discover that it's a fair bargain. The proof of this is that nobody who knows how to do this would go back and trade the new knowledge to get the x number of hours back. Knowledge trumps ignorance every time. Why choose black and white when we can have color and high def?

Fourth, It Gets Easier

It gets easier because your knowledge base is cumulative. Say you learn enough stuff to make a valid exegesis of a single passage. When you turn to a different passage, you don't forget what you learned about the first one; you carry that forward. If something that was relevant there turns out to be relevant here, you don't have to discover it all over again. What you're doing is growing schemas, sometimes with great effort, but each new thread of information makes the subsequent information easier to grasp. Each new detail you learn makes you a better exegete for the material you have yet to study.

Fifth, You're Not Alone

In chapter 3, I said that exegesis is collegial. Here let me reinforce that with the comment that we have at our disposal a whole body of literature, created and preserved for us by earnest and thoughtful interpreters who have been at this task for nearly two thousand years. We're also not alone because we have the resources of the living church to assist us. Finally, we're not alone because the Holy Spirit, who inspired the text in the first place, comes alongside us and assists us in our work.

And a Couple of Challenges . . .

I'd also like to leave you with a couple of challenges.

First, There's Still More to Learn about Early Christianity

In chapter 2, I set out the problem of hermeneutics with a diagram:

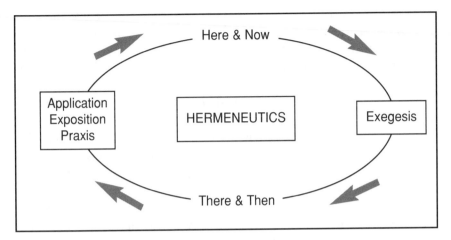

Figure 18.1

In this book, we've covered the basic steps of the first half of that journey. The disciplines we've surveyed are what I have called the *primary disciplines* of exegesis. These are the disciplines necessary to get at what the authors of the Bible intended by what they wrote—there and then.

But is it possible to uncover other information, information that the authors did *not* intend but that may be valid and important in its own right? Most NT scholars think it is. Suppose my sink springs a leak. I call a plumber. When she arrives, she tells me she's come to fix my "facet," using that dry twang you usually associate with a New England accent. She may not be intending to tell me she's from New England, but she tells me anyway in her diction and pronunciation. (If she said she'd heard that my faucet "needed fixin'," I'd know she was from somewhere in the upper Midwest.)

We can do this with the NT too but we have to refocus our attention if we expect to get it right, which means using a different set of paradigms. (These have technical names like *Redaction Criticism, Source Criticism, Audience Criticism* and so forth. An advanced level of *Form Criticism* fits in this category too.) I call these the *secondary disciplines* of exegesis. We can learn a lot by reading between the lines. They're secondary because they pretty much depend on both the logic and the results of the primary disciplines to make sense. Much of the academic debate about historical Jesus is carried on at the level of the secondary disciplines, which means that the debate itself is rough sledding until we master the basic skills of exegesis.

By and large, the secondary disciplines use the text as a way of focusing on the factors that gave rise to the text. That is, they reconstruct the sources that the authors used, and then using those sources, they reconstruct the historical factors that may have shaped the author's decisions about what to include and where to put it. When we study these things, scholars say we are looking at the world *behind* the text, rather than at the text itself.

Along the way, when we study the world behind the text, we may discover that our findings reinforce, expand, nuance, or correct the conclusions we reached using the primary disciplines. We can learn a lot by reading between the lines. So we have the possibility of secondary corroboration, much the way text critics seek corroboration by solving the problem of the manuscripts using two different disciplines (*internal transcriptional probability* and *external manuscript evidence*—remember?). But first things first. To borrow a phrase from C. S. Lewis, it makes little sense to read between the lines unless first we read the lines themselves. The secondary disciplines of exegesis are rightly the subject of another study.

I hope you've realized too that we're still learning about the daily life in the ancient world. As new discoveries come to light, they may shed new light on early Christian beliefs and patterns of life, so each new discovery has the potential to improve our understanding of what the Bible *meant*—there and then.

Second, There's Still More to Learn about What the Bible *Means Today—Here and Now*

We also have more to learn about what the Bible means today. This is the second movement of hermeneutics—the part scholars call *praxis*, *exposition*, or *application*. Once we've figured out what the text meant to its original writers and readers, we still have to ask what it means here and now, two thousand years later, in a world the original writers and readers of the Bible could hardly have imagined.

One way of refining our thinking about such things is to study the way earlier generations of Christian readers have understood the Bible, what they thought were its theological, ethical, and pastoral implications, or to probe the impact of the Bible on the history of art and music. The history of interpretation may call attention to details in the text we may have overlooked or discounted, or provide clues about what Christians in different times and places brought with them to the reading. What we're studying here is the *impact* of the text. In a sense, this is the opposite of getting *behind* the text, so scholars call this the world *in front of* the text. How we do that is also the subject of another study.

And in the End, a Grace

If there's a takeaway value for this book, it's this: There is more to the Bible than meets the eye. And if there's a takeaway value for this chapter, it's that there is yet more to learn as we explore that something more about the Bible. Not only can we study the text itself, but we can study the world *behind* the text and the world *in front of* the text. But a faithful reading of the Bible suggests that there is something more still. There is also a reality that comes to us from *beyond* the text.

My colleague Russ Spittler tells a story about a moment of sudden clarity that came to him over Saturday morning coffee. He had read that all packaged food sold in the United States must have the ingredients clearly displayed on the label. Curious, he picked up the empty wrapper of his morning bread, and began reading off the ingredients that were printed on the clear plastic of the wrapper: Wheat flour, barley flour, iron, niacin, thiamin, wheat gluten. . . .

He was engrossed in this task when one of his daughters burst into the room, running to him with outstretched arms, calling out, "Daddy, Daddy, Daddy." He looked up to see her, but he saw her coming to him through the wording of the ingredients list on the bread package.

So it is with the Word of God. Even as we immerse ourselves in the text, if we attune our sensitivities right we see also that beyond the text there comes to us One who loves us, who calls us by name, who comes to us, as it were, *through* the text, arms outstretched. To see that One, we need more than accurate information; we need insight. And we do not invite insight only by developing more and better exegetical skills. We invite insight by nurturing both open hearts and daring minds.

Notes

1. Reading the Bible and Aching for God

1. Peter J. Gomes, *The Good Book: Reading the Bible with Mind and Heart* (San Francisco: Harper, 2002), 12.

2. Sam Keen, *To a Dancing God* (New York: Harper & Row, 1970), 100.

3. Ibid, 101.

4. Ibid.

5. Ibid.

6. James Michener, *The Fires of Spring* (New York: Random House, 1949), 488.

7. Peter Berger, *The Heretical Imperative* (Garden City, N.J.: Anchor Books/Doubleday, 1979), 184.

8. Stanley Hauerwas, *A Community of Character: Toward a Constructive Christian Social Ethic* (Notre Dame: University of Notre Dame Press, 1981), 1.

2. It Isn't Just about God; It's also about Garry

1. Almost certainly he would not, on the grounds that such a thing is unnatural.

3. The Bible Says It; I Believe It; That Settles It—Oh, Really?

1. The verse is ambiguous in the King James Bible, but the Greek is quite clear. More recent translators have cleared up the ambiguity this way: "Drink from it, all of you" (NASB, NIV), "Drink this, all of you" (*The Message*), "Drink of it, all of you" (RSV).

2. Simpson replied with a theological discussion of Gen 2:21-22: "So the LORD God caused a deep sleep to fall upon the man, and while he slept took one of his ribs and closed up its place with flesh; and the rib which the LORD God had taken from the man he made into a woman and brought her to the man."

Simpson's argument carried the day, and the use of chloroform came into common use, even among Christians.

3. Thomas Kuhn, *The Structure of Scientific Revolutions* (Chicago: University of Chicago Press, 1970).

4. Reconstructing the Original Wording

1. Larry Hurtado, *Mark* (NICB; Peabody, Mass.: Hendrickson, 1989), 289.

5. Your Version, My Version

1. Garry Trudeau, "I Am a Tip-Top Startlet," *Time* (May 20, 1996): 84.

6. The Master Paradigm

1. D. R. Dooling and R. Lachman, "Effects of Comprehension on Retention of Prose," *Journal of Experimental Psychology* 88 (1971): 216-22.

2. Richard Lederer, *Anguished English: An Anthology of Accidental Assaults Upon Our Language* (Charleston: Wyrick & Company, 1987), 56-66.

3. I have no idea where this is from. Someone sent it as an e-mail. If you're looking for a reference here, you're out of luck. Sorry.

7. How We Fill in Gaps

1. Umberto Eco, *The Role of the Reader: Explorations in the Semiotics of Texts* (Bloomington: Indiana University Press, 1979), 18.

2. There is a physiological reason for the loss of detail: The mind can manage only a small number of details at a time. See George Miller, "The Magical Number Seven, Plus or Minus Two: Some Limits on Our Capacity for Processing Information," *Psychological Review* 63 (1956): 81-97.

3. If you respond with, "Anybody got a peanut?" you know already about gap-filling based on cultural information.

4. Richard C. White, "Preaching Between the Lines," in *The Best in Theology: Volume Two*, ed. Paul Fromer (Carol Stream, Ill. Christianity Today, n.d.): 419-21.

5. Ibid.

6. Ibid.

7. Notice that I didn't say who Gordon Fee is. Strictly speaking, while we're reading, the name *Gordon Fee* also functions as a schema.

10. How We Find Out about Cultural Norms

1. Kenneth Good, *Into the Heart: One Man's Pursuit of Love and Knowledge among the Yanomama* (New York: Simon & Schuster, 1991).

2. I wrote a book about this once. See: Jerry Camery-Hoggatt, *Grapevine: The Spirituality of Gossip* (Scottdale, Pa.: Herald Press, 2002).

12. How We Find Out about Historical Contexts

1. Werner Georg Kümmel, *Introduction to the New Testament*, trans. Howard Clark Kee (Nashville: Abingdon Press: 1973), 28.

13. How We Disambiguate

1. From *Games Magazine* (January 1984).
2. Patricia Carpenter and Meredyth Daneman, "Lexical Retrieval and Error Recovery in Reading: A Model Based on Eye Fixations," *Journal of Verbal Learning and Verbal Behavior* 20 (1981): 137-60.
3. J. D. Bransford and M. K. Johnson, "Considerations of Some Problems of Comprehension" (paper presented at the eighth Carnegie Conference on Cognition, May 1971).

14. How We Recognize Polyvalence

1. This song is by Bobby Boyd, Warren Dale Haynes, and Dennis Robbins; it appears on Garth Brooks's *Friends in Low Places* album, ©1993, Garthart, Inc. Used by permission.
2. Luis Alonso Schökel, "Hermeneutics in the Light of Language and Literature," *Catholic Biblical Quarterly* 25 (1963): 380.
3. I have taken over the term *overcode* from Umberto Eco, *The Role of the Reader: Explorations in the Semiotics of Texts* (Bloomington: Indiana University Press, 1984), 19.
4. J. R. Stroop, "Studies of Interference in Serial Verbal Reactions," *Journal of Experimental Psychology* 18 (1935): 643-62.
5. For this I am indebted to Herbert Clark and Eve Clark, *Psychology and Language: An Introduction to Psycholinguistics* (New York: Harcourt Brace Jovanovich, 1977), 81.
6. Elton Trueblood, *The Humor of Christ* (New York: Harper & Row, 1964).
7. There's a popular interpretation of this passage that understands "eye of the needle" to refer to a "gate within the gate" of an oriental city. This is largely fanciful. A second approach is based on the fact that the Greek words for "camel" and for "rope" differ by a single letter—*kamelos//kamilos*—a coincidence that is exploited by a few late manuscripts ($f^{13,28}$) at Mark 10:25. (Perhaps Jesus really said "rope.") Against both of these possibilities, we must note there are numerous rabbinic parallels suggesting that what is in view is a literal camel and a literal needle (on which see William Lane, *The Gospel According to Mark* [NIC; Grand Rapids: Eerdmans, 1974]: 369f.). This is, according to Jakob Jonsson, an example of "excellent paradoxical humour" (*Humour and Irony in the New Testament Illuminated by Parallels in Talmud and Midrash* [1965; reissue, Leiden: Brill, 1985], 110).
8. Frederick Buechner, *Wishful Thinking: A Theological ABC* (New York: Harper and Row, 1973), 81.
9. Halford Luccock, in *Christian Century* (Feb. 17, 1960): 207.

15. How We Deal with Intertextuality

1. Robert Alter, *The Art of Biblical Narrative* (New York: Basic Books, 1981), 50f.
2. One interpreter urges caution: Jesus isn't so much accusing her as "naming her wound."
3. Dinesh D'Souza, *Illiberal Education: The Politics of Race and Sex on Campus* (New York: Free Press, 1991), 1.
4. The rhetorical effect of allusions is more potent than that of quotations, precisely because quotations are more focused, call for a different type of readerly work, and are not overcoded on top of the primary frame.

5. In his defense, Henley was an accomplished poet, writer, and editor who enriched the world by sponsoring young literary talents, but he did so against enormous personal odds—an amputated leg and the lingering after-effects of tuberculosis. He wrote "Invictus" from a hospital bed. Good for him, I say.

16. How We Deal with Sequence and Pace

1. A. J. Sanford and S. C. Garrod, *Understanding Written Language* (New York: John Wiley & Sons, 1981), 114.

2. While the literary critics have widely recognized this reality, they have employed an equally wide range of terms to describe it. A. A. Mendilow (*Time and the Novel* [New York: Humanities Press, 1952]: 65-71) distinguished between "chronological time" and "fictional time"; Gerard Genette (*Narrative Discourse: An Essay in Method* [Ithaca, N.Y.: Cornell University Press, 1980]: 33-86) distinguished between "story time" and "narrative time." Seymour Chatman (*Story and Discourse* [Ithaca, N.Y.: Cornell University Press, 1978], 62f) distinguished between "story time" and "discourse time." I have learned the most about this topic from Menakhem Perry, "Literary Dynamics: How the Order of a Text Creates Its Meanings," *Poetics Today* 1 (1979): 35-64.

3. Paul Kolers, "Some Psychological Aspects of Pattern Recognition," in *Recognizing Patterns*, ed. P. Kolers and M. Eden (Cambridge, Mass.: MIT Press, 1968). For an extensive discussion of related literature, see M. T. Turvey, "Constructive Theory, Perceptual Systems, and Tacit Knowledge," in *Cognition and the Symbolic Processes*, ed. W. B. Weimer and D. S. Palermo (Hillsdale, N.J.: Erlbaum, 1974), 165-80.

4. This is especially so if, as is sometimes argued, the expression *paradothenai* here means "to be handed over to execution." This possibility is suggested by Mark's grammar, and—remember—Mark's reader would not have had the other Gospels around to suggest otherwise.

5. James L. Resseguie, "Reader-Response Criticism and Synoptic Gospels," *Journal of the American Academy of Religion* 52 (1984): 314.

6. Ibid. Jeffery Staley describes a similar phenomenon under the term "victimization" in John 4 (*The Print's First Kiss: A Rhetorical Investigation of the Implied Reader in the Fourth Gospel* [SBLDS 82; Atlanta: Scholars Press, 1988]: 95-118), and Andrew Lincoln offers this reversal of expectations as a fundamental aspect of the irony that ends Mark's Gospel ("The Promise and the Failure: Mark 16:7, 8," *Journal of Biblical Literature* 108 [1989]: 290f).

7. Laurence Perrine, *Story and Structure* (New York: Harcourt, Brace and World, 1959), 66.

8. Menakhem Perry, "Literary Dynamics: How the Order of a Text Creates Its Meanings [With an Analysis of Faulkner's "A Rose for Emily]," *Poetics Today* 1 (1979): 41.

17. Pulling It All Together

1. This is the term commonly translated *Scribe*.

2. What about sojourners? Leviticus 19 goes on to use identical language for one's responsibilities to the sojourner in the land: "You shall treat him as a native among you, and you shall love him as yourself" (v. 34). But the very fact that the sojourner is singled

out in this way means that in v. 18 the term "neighbor" cannot be automatically general-ized to mean "fellow human being." If it is a closely limited term there, then the respon-sibilities to sojourners defined in v. 34 cannot be generalized either. Later rabbinic thought specifically understood "sojourner" to refer to full proselytes and in that way restricted Leviticus 19:34 to exclude the traveler who simply passed through the land. Samaritans were excluded, too, as were resident aliens who do not join the community within twelve months (see *Mekilta Exodus 21:35*). On this see Johannes Fichtner, "*Plesion*" in *Theological Dictionary of the New Testament* (ed. G. Kittel and G. Friedrich, trans. G. Bromiley: Grand Rapids: Eerdmans, 1968) 6:315.

3. Eta Linnemann, *Jesus of the Parables* (New York: Harper & Row, 1966), 51: "All ancient cultures draw a line between insiders and outsiders, and one set of laws applies for dealing with those inside and another for those outside."

4. Note that there is a formally similar beginning in the context of a theological debate between Jesus and the Sadducees about resurrection from the dead (Luke 20:27-34 = Mark 12:18-27). There, after stating the Mosaic regulation on the law of levirate mar-riage, they pose a hypothetical case. That case begins like this story: "Now there were seven brothers..." (v. 29).

5. Apparently the safety of travelers was a serious and widespread concern. Adolf Deissmann (*Light from the Ancient Near East* [1927, reprint: Peabody, Mass.: Hendrickson, 1995], 134) records a letter written about 171 CE, found at Euhemeria, in which pig mer-chants report having been waylaid on the road. The parallels with the story of the Samaritan are striking, though of course, only of limited exegetical value:

> Yesterday, which was the 19th of the present month of Thoth, as we were return-ing about daybreak from the village of Theadelphia in the division of Themistes, certain malefactors came upon us between Polydeucia and Theadelphia, and bound us, with the guard of the tower also, and assaulted us with many stripes, and wounded Pasion, and robbed us of 1 pig, and carried off Pasion's coat.

6. J. Duncan M. Derrett, "Law in the New Testament" Fresh Light on the Parable of the Good Samaritan." *New Testament Studies* 11 (1964): 25-26.

7. J. M. Furness, "Fresh Light on Luke 10:25-37," *Expository Times* 80 (1969): 182.

8. This is the core of the story as L. Paul Trudinger understands it: "For the question 'Which one was neighbor to the man who was waylaid' requires that the answer be given from the position of the man in trouble; that the lawyer put himself in the place of the waylaid man; that he answer as one in need of help ("Once Again, Now, 'Who Is My Neighbor?'" *Evangelical Quarterly* 48 [1976], 161).

9. The technical term here is *irenicon*.

18. Looking Ahead, Looking Beyond

1. Thomas Howard, *Christ the Tiger: A Postscript to Dogma* (Philadelphia: Lippincott, 1967), 9-10.

Index of Scripture

Index of Names

Alter, Robert, 177-78, 202, 229

Bacon, Sir Francis, 31
Bailey, James, 137
Bar-Efrat, Shimon, 202
Barr, David, 150
Berkley, T. W., 185
Ben Sirach, 59
Berger, Peter, 13, 227
Bierce, Ambrose, 189, 190, 197
Boyd, Bobby, 229
Brooks, Garth, 165, 229
Bransford, J. D., 160, 229
Bromiley, Geoffrey, 105
Buechner, Frederick, 229
Byrne, Robert, 181

Camery-Hoggatt, Jerry, 228
Camp, Hamilton, 143
Carpenter, Patricia, 157-58, 229
Carson, D. A., 105
Cato, Marcus Porcius, 129
Chatman, Seymour, 230
Clark, Eve, 229
Clark, Herbert, 229
Copernicus, Nicholas, 31

Daneman, Meredyth, 157-58, 229
Danker, Frederick, 105
Dawn, Marva, 122-23
Day, Dorothea, 183
Deissmann, Adolf, 231
Derrett, J. Duncan, M., 210, 231

Dooling, D. R., 77, 208
Doyle, Arthur Conan, 100-1
D'Souza, Dinesh, 179, 229

Eco, Umberto, 85, 228, 229
Ehrman, Bart, 57
Einstein, Albert, 74
Eliot, T. S., 179, 181
Ellington, John, 185
Elliott, John, 126

Fee, Gordon, 57, 202
Fergusen, Everett, 112
Fewell, D. N., 185
Friedrich, Gerhard, 105
Furness, J. M., 231

Garrod, S. C., 230
Genette, Gerard, 230
Gomes, Peter, 6, 227
Good, Kenneth, 116, 228
Graham, Billy, 63
Grisham, John, 130

Handey, Jack, 78, 102, 104
Harvey, Paul, 189
Hauerwas, Stanley, 14, 227
Hawking, Stephen, 74
Hayes, Richard B., 185
Haynes, Warren, 229
Henley, William Ernest, 183
Hodges, Zane, 57
Holladay, Carl, 150

Index of Subjects